On Mothers

TRUE STORIES OF LAUGHTER, LONGING, AND LOVE

Edited by Edward McCann

Read650 • 1 Writer. 5 Minutes. 650 Words.

Founder / Editor • Edward McCann
Executive Producer • Richard Kollath
Senior Editor / Literary Ombudsman • Steven Lewis
Editor • Karen Dukess
Editor • David Masello
Editor • Lisa Donati Mayer
Copy Editor • Shelley Sandler Kenney
Marketing/Communications • Jane Kaupp
Design Director • Diane Fokas
Technical Advisor • Conrad Trautmann
Technical Advisor • Stephen Kaupp
Director of Photography • Kevin O'Connor
Chief Audio Engineer • Jesse Chason
Intern • Kerry Lubman
Intern • Olivia Prestia

Advisory Committee
Sara Caldwell, Richard Kollath, Steven Lewis, David Masello,
Irene O'Garden, John Pielmeier, Susan Ragusa, James Russek,
Angela Derecas Taylor

"If you bungle raising your children,
I don't think whatever else you do well matters very much."

—*Jacqueline Kennedy Onassis*

The English novelist and poet Mary Ann Evans (writing under the pen name George Eliot) wrote, "Life began with waking up and loving my mother's face."

For most of us, our mother *is* our first love. She is also, for a time, our entire world, serving as our protector, nurturer, and teacher. Our relationships with our mothers is both simple and elemental, arugably the most important one there is. Yet there may also be times when it is the most fraught and complicated relationship we'll ever know.

The work in the pages that follow is a wide ranging survey of mothers, mothering, and motherlessness, from an exceptional group of essayists, and I'm proud to present their personal stories to you.

Read650 is a literary nonprofit promoting writers through live and digital performances that celebrate the spoken word—a forum organized around single, broad topics featuring 650-word personal stories that can be performed in five minutes. The recorded performances from our events are added to a growing archive of writers reading their work aloud, with additional planned exposure through podcasts, broadcasts, our YouTube channel, and in printed volumes like the one you hold in your hand.

At Read650 we showcase writers of all ages with good stories to tell, and first-timers often share the stage with bestselling authors. It's all about the writing—word choices, the shape of sentences and paragraphs, the arc of a narrative, and the poetry of a unique literary voice. To submit your work or attend our shows, visit our website or Facebook page, and join our mailing list. Tell your friends about us, and please help spread the word about the spoken word.

Ed McCann

Edward McCann, Founder / Editor

READ650.ORG
FACEBOOK.COM/READ650

CONTENTS

CONTENTS

On Mothers

TRUE STORIES OF LAUGHTER, LONGING, AND LOVE

ZEA ARCHER

Zea Archer is a writer and librarian living in Northern New Jersey. Her poems, plays, and reviews have been read and performed in queer spaces, including Skin to Skin, Your Name Here, and The Lesbrary. Her nonfiction work on (impending) queer motherhood appears in *Hot Metal Bridge*, Santa Fe Writers Project Quarterly, and *Musepaper*.

THE STORK

Zea Archer

It's really just a glorified cervical cap. Insistently unsexy, it's a decided improvement on the penis which, I suppose, tries. It's meant for intra-vaginal insemination, which sounds like regular insemination because it is. With specimen cup locked in and plunger in place, semen is deposited at the terminus of the cervix and kept corked for up to six hours, after which it is neatly pulled out of the vaginal canal like a tampon. Its precision and functionality do take a lot of the spontaneity out of the attempt at conception—not to mention some of the fun. "The Stork" isn't a sex toy. It's all work and no play, and we are in the business of getting pregnant.

For a large chunk of whatever time it is normal to begin thinking about these things, I was certain I didn't want to be a parent. My distaste for parenthood was nurtured by my increasing and not wholly unwelcome belief that I would spend my life alone.

It was generally understood that to be gay was to be single; maybe "partnered," but never "parent." Then, at twenty-one, I fell in love. Being in love can change a lot of things about a person. For me, it softened me in ways I so desperately needed to be softened. The magic of falling in love cracked open possibility. Yet our desire for parenthood remains a disruption. To some, we're "playing god." To others, we're shamelessly conceding defeat to heteronormativity. Honestly, if someone is asking to spend the foreseeable future elbow-deep in feces and vomit, why stop them?

We are two months away from our first go at it—our first walk around the block while our friend ushers his raw genetic material into a cervical cap; our first time loading the plunger, inserting, and releasing; our first time squealing with delight at the done deed, while I lie level with her midsection and imagine the cellular activity taking place; our first time waiting an agonizing two weeks, while she feels every cramp and twitch like never before; the first pregnancy test, or first disappointing period; and first time waiting two weeks to try it all again.

While a majority of the reviews bubble and exclaim about The Stork delivering on the first attempt, I can't help but temper my expectations. I'm putting my faith—my future—in a non-reusable applicator device, a piece of $59.99 plastic on the shelf at CVS.

What will it mean to help someone conceive? I am filling a space rarely occupied—a third person in the room in which sperm and ovum meet. I will be the vessel through which the seed of life bursts open. I will carry the specimen cup with holy reverence up the stairs and observe her prostrate before the life-giving altar, a supine woman on a bed. I will gently guide the applicator through a reverse trip into the birth canal, and I will plunge the petals open and deliver to the mighty cervix an offering, tens of millions of offerings. I will say a blessing as the journey commences and my work as interlocutor concludes: Godspeed, boys.

This is the origin story of so many lives, and yet so few, and still entirely its own. Who am I to the life begun here? A middle-man? Technically unnecessary? Just a big kid playing God with sperm and egg?— dare I say: a parent?

As the great work begins—in a uterine tube, in the body of a woman I love, maybe while sleeping, or running, or on an airplane—I will be ready for the labor. Used to plunging—feet first, cap erect, and with abandon—I will dive into this new life. If I was good enough to be God for a moment, I'll be good enough for whatever is next.

KATE BASSETT

Kate Bassett is an executive assistant at the San Francisco Symphony. A former student of the San Francisco Conservatory of Music, she enjoyed several careers before landing at the symphony, including international fashion modelling, prenatal health education, and advertising. An on-again/off-again violinist, she has recently developed a preference for the pen over the bow, and writes about her life, her family, and her travels. She finds joy in making collages, walking through old-growth redwood forests, and attempting to master the French language. She is currently working on a memoir. You can find her on Twitter at @KatherineTudor.

THE YEAR

Kate Bassett

It was November and I was sitting in my apartment in Oakland; my mother, in Arizona, on the other end of the line. I remember her voice wrapping around my ears like a thick fog as she said the words: "I am dying." The weight of the phone suddenly heavy—the hand that held it, numb. "I am dying," she repeated, this time in a deeper color—one that obscured my vision until I blinked it away.

She was telling me why. She was telling me what happened. The doctors and the information they gave her—names and dates and explanations; parts of the body—and she was telling me with a voice that brought me back to my childhood and made me feel small and powerless. It was a voice of misplaced rage that carried the weight of the past.

She was dying of cirrhosis of the liver and she had been told she would be gone within the year. We were on the phone for what felt like hours, but beyond some facts she relayed and the tone she carried, our conversation would vanish from my memory. Shock has a funny way of scrambling the mind. I thought about all of the years of drinking and how her body was paying attention. I thought about all the times I tried to understand her anger, and always thought it was my fault.

Over the next several months she switched back and forth between telling me she was dying and denying it. I became her medical liaison, I became her power of attorney, I became the one the paramedics called; I became grown-up. I was the only one in the family left who would speak to her; the only one who would go see her; the only one. I tried to reckon with the fact that she was so many contrasting elements to me: comfort and sorrow, protection and pain, beauty and heartbreak. Mother and alcoholic.

She came to California for the last time in May and I drove her down to Santa Cruz to see her friends. No one was saying that it was goodbye, but that is exactly what it was. No one commented on how frail she was and how her eyes were like a flickering flame. We made a stop at her favorite beach and found a spot on the sand. She was cold despite the warm sun, so I wrapped her in my cardigan and fussed with the buttons until she was secure. We were silent amidst the noise between us, while we watched the waves come and go and come again. She took a picture of me with my disposable camera, which I would later develop. The photo had her finger in it, like a fuzzy spirit in the corner of the frame.

There were so many phone calls that year. In August I got the final one. Somehow my body moved miles across cities and states, and I was there with her in her bedroom with the family photos on her dresser, and the card I sent her on her shelf, and the book she was reading on her nightstand. I held her head and stroked her hair, and she said to me "you are so good." I felt something shift in a deep place in my heart. A few days later she was gone.

Back in my apartment in Oakland, I picked up the phone to call her. Magical thinking. If she had answered, I might have said "why did you do this to yourself?" I might have said "how could you do this to me?" I might have said, "I miss you so much." Instead, the phone rang on—the silence between tones, deafening. I put down the receiver and walked into the summer night, where the sky was turning indigo.

ELVA BENNETT

Elva Bennett is a climate science professional and writer from North Carolina who currently resides in Brooklyn, New York. Elva studies climate dynamics and works in climate change adaptation. They hold an MA in climate and society from Columbia University and a BS in environmental science from the University of North Carolina at Chapel Hill.

EMERGENCY CONTACT

Elva Bennett

I came out to mom as gender non-binary in a letter, post-marked from New York City to Greensboro, North Carolina. I figured a letter offered the time to consult my stepfather and Google, something that a conversation might not afford.

She called after that grace period and said mostly the right things, albeit with the brevity and stiffness of unfamiliarity. The first of many stilted conversations, filled with base support, but lacking curiosity or enthusiasm.

The harder phone call came later, when I told her about top surgery.

In the months between, I had found a surgeon, verified insurance coverage, secured medical-necessity letters, and scheduled my surgery—all in secret.

Usually, Mom is first and last consultant on all major life decisions; but now, I hadn't called for advice; instead, I called to tell her that I had gone through the hardest and scariest thing I've ever done without her, intentionally.

I hadn't told anyone, save a few friends, but keeping it from Mom was the hardest—and the most necessary.

Coming to terms with my gender was an exercise in shutting out everything that society ever told me about what gender is and who I could be. It was uncomfortable, terrifying, and joyful, but more than anything, it was exhausting.

I spent months navigating a transphobic healthcare system while seeking surgery. This left me emotionally raw and fragile, and I was afraid a well-meaning but misguided comment from Mom would send me over the edge. So I kept her in the dark.

Trying to protect myself in the great big binary, cisgender world meant boundaries came down hard and fast and everywhere.

I denied Mom the opportunity to misspeak and unwittingly get lumped in with all I was up against, but with it, I denied her the opportunity to be on my side.

Instead, I brought her a seamless plan, my surgical transition bundled up in a neat and complete package.

She felt blindsided.

In the same conversation in which she asked me to wait to have surgery, she told me if I insisted on doing it now, she would come. She would be there to take care of me.

If I waited at all, it would only be for her to catch up.

I told her she wasn't allowed to come. Another blow. But I couldn't wake up after surgery, back in my body, and see doubt on anyone's face, especially hers.

My best friend already had a plane ticket, someone I could count on to get pronouns right every time and treat surgery like the celebration it was.

The day United Healthcare called to say my insurance plan had a special clause, denying coverage for any gender-affirming surgery, was the worst day of my life.

In a spectacular case of bad timing, I got this call on the first day of a new job.

I stood outside my office building, crying, and called mom.

We were both hurting from different wounds, but my perfect plan was unraveling and hers was the only cellular shoulder I wanted to cry on. I held the phone to my face as I gasped for air between loud and uncontrollable sobs.

She had never heard me like that. This is the woman who knew the meaning behind the different tenors of my cry as a baby, and I guess she still did because something switched for her then—she went from asking if I was sure to reassuring me that this will happen for you. If it doesn't happen now, it will happen next year, and now you don't have to do it alone.

And it did happen for me. There were many more tearful phone calls. There still are.

But there were no tears on the day of surgery – that day was all smiles, and mom was there for it.

ANN CASAPINI

Ann Casapini has been a yoga and meditation instructor since 1995. She also loves to write, sing and dance salsa! She has been published in the 2020 *Crack the Spine* anthology, specifically in its *Neighbors* edition; and the *Still Point Arts Quarterly* that focuses on the theme of The Dance. Her writing has also appeared in *Dunes Review; The Sun*; and *Awakened Voices* Blog and its extension, *The Nightingale*. Ann is a repeat contributor to both Read650 and Military Experience & the Arts' online journal. Ann studies writing with Steven Lewis and lives in Tuckahoe, New York.

WHO IS SHE?

Ann Casapini

My ninety-two-year-old mother is visiting with me this week. She gets up from the couch and stumbles. I run over to assist, but miraculously, she finds her footing before I reach her side.

Who is this woman? I can't reconcile the image of my strong mother that I have in my mind with this tottering woman in front of me, weighing less than a hundred pounds. How could this be the same woman who, all on her own, dragged her four young children, plus five suitcases, to her birthplace, Colombia, in 1964, just to prove a point to my father?

It's mid-afternoon. Mom is reading the newspaper. Fifteen minutes later, I see her sleeping in an awkward position, folded onto the dining room table, with her head on her forearms.

"Mom...Mama...would you like to lie down on the couch?"

She sits up. "No, I'm not tired! What did I do today? Just sit and eat."

She swears she never naps but soon after her "bocadillo a media tarde" (afternoon snack) I find her dozing again, this time curled up on my big comfy armchair. I tuck a pillow under her head and place a blanket over her.

I've pleaded with her to let us help her sell her Long Island home and move closer to us, but she refuses. She is so strong-willed, my father used to call her "La Senora: The Boss Lady."

We have a dinner party, and my nephew-in-law Eugenio sits next to my mom. Eugenio seems to easily engage her, talking in Spanish. I see her nodding her head and smiling again and again. On his way out, he tells me he has invited my mother to go visit his Dominican aunts in the Bronx and that he'll pick her up the next day atone-thirty.

At breakfast the following morning I speak to my mother about the plan.

"Mama, are you looking forward to visiting with Eugenio's aunts today?"

She tilts her head and looks at me like I am crazy.

"What are you talking about? Eugenio didn't mention his aunts. I'd certainly know if I got an invitation. He sat right next to me the entire evening."

I can't contain my gasp. She must have been pretending to understand the entire conversation. Or worse…Oh God, could she have already forgotten? I go into the kitchen to get more coffee and try to hide my concern. She has always prided herself in remembering details. She was the one who knew every family member's birthday, and even everyone's anniversary!

The sun is out today so I suggest to Mom we go for a walk around the block. She resists at first, apprehensive of the cold, yet I know she used to love to walk in all seasons. We used to play tourist in New York City. She would walk at such a speed I'd have to run to keep up with her. I used to call her my "Energizer Bunny." She agrees to go just to the corner.

I help her find her scarf, gloves and loafers. Then I see she has no socks. It's November, thirty-five degrees, and she didn't think she'd need them. I run upstairs and grab a warm pair. She doesn't know how to dress properly anymore. Even packing a small suitcase for a week's visit with me overwhelms her.

As we walk, I notice her favorite pair of loafers are falling apart. I know she has at least six other pairs, but I ask, "Mama, are these your only pair of loafers?"

"Umm...yes. Anyway, they're comfortable and it doesn't matter, since I don't know anyone in your neighborhood."

Who is this woman? My mother always used to care about how she dressed when out of the house.

I am sad and scared and missing my younger mom. There is nothing to do but swallow back my tears and hold her hand.

MARY GRACE COLANGELO

Mary Grace Colangelo is a corporate leadership and communication coach, turned writer, who lives in Bronxville, New York with her husband, son, and two stepsons. Central to her writing is the complexity and comedy of domestic relationships, inspired by her own experience growing up in a large, Irish-Catholic family, the acquisition of her husband's enormous first-generation Italian family, and her transition into stepmothering and co-parenting. She is enrolled at The Writing Institute at Sarah Lawrence College and hopes to finish her first novel later this year.

EVERYTHING AND NOTHING

Mary Grace Colangelo

I obsess over what she did in the moments just before. I imagine her moving through their big, empty home like a ghost, touching things for the last time: the coffee pot, the counter, the sink, my piano. We know she collected the recycling container from the curb; the everyday-ness of this is laughable considering the monumental finality of what she did next.

I wonder what she was wearing. I wonder if she savored her coffee or if she let it grow cold on the nightstand. But most of all, like a desperate child, I wonder if she thought of us: of my father, and my sisters, and my brother, and me. I lay awake at night and wonder if she thought of me in the moments before she took all that was left of her pills: one bottle for insomnia, one bottle for anxiety and one half-bottle for depression.

My dad found her unconscious on the floor, her pulse faint, but there. He texted us as he sped behind the ambulance. He asked us not to call, said it was touch and go and he'd tell us more when he could. We fell apart on the other ends of our phones, jerked from the comfort of our Friday mornings, no longer absorbed with our kids, our husbands, our jobs, our lives. How could we have let it get this bad? This strong, frustrating fireball didn't burn out overnight. Hadn't we cared that she had grown so faint she was barely there?

It took her two days to wake up and when she did, we begged her to tell us that this was an accident. Instead, she told us she wanted to die because she had nothing left. Each one of her eight children had moved away, condemning her to a loneliness that turned into insomnia, that turned into depression, that turned into suicide. I choked on my greedy sobs and tried to forget that the night before she had FaceTimed with my husband, my two-year-old, and me. My sweet son, he wiped my tears.

I flew to Florida and spent a week fighting to get her out of the psych ward. I yelled at the incompetent social workers, secretly grateful for someone to hate because I was so, so mad that she wasn't trying. I did research, made phone calls and went on runs where, miles from their house, I fell to my knees and screamed. Six days later, we drove her to an inpatient facility where she would spend the next thirty days, journaling, practicing yoga, attending one-on-one and group therapy sessions. In the back of my dad's Rav4, she rocked and cried and begged us to take her home. She didn't notice when I flicked the childproof locks.

It has been one year. She's not suicidal, but I'm not sure if that's because she's better or because she's sedated. My dad flies her across the country so she can be at all of the appropriate events: baptisms, graduations, wedding dress shopping. She is shy and cautious, and she hasn't stopped rocking. I tell people she had a stroke because the truth is humiliating. If you met her now, you'd think she was a nothing person.

But, my God, if you knew her before, she was an everything person. She had opinions and fire in her belly. She got on the floor to play with her grandchildren, she laughed and sang in Spanish. She could be exhausting. She sucked the energy out of the room without even trying, but I'd willingly stand by and let her do it today, if only she could.

I try to forgive the universe, and my dad, and myself, and most of all, her. She did the best that she could, and even if she didn't, because she couldn't, she is still my mom, and I love her, and I'm sorry.

MOIRA COLANGELO

Moira Colangelo is a retired healthcare executive who is an avid hiker, cook, and reader. She discovered the Writing Institute at Sarah Lawrence College two years ago and found flash fiction a great way to share short stories about her large Irish family as well as other life experiences from her travels.

MOVING ON

Moira Colangelo

With five out of seven children living near my parents in Connecticut, it made no sense to me when my mother decided that she and dad would move six-hundred miles away to North Carolina where my youngest sister lives. My mother recited her reasons: better weather, less taxes, a house without stairs. I countered with offers and schemes to keep them local. It just made no sense to me and as often as I got the chance, I told my mother so.

My sister Sharon and I had the dubious privilege of spending a week that summer of 2005 helping pack or dispose of forty plus years of my elderly parents' belongings. For the third day in a row we carry, roll, and drag boxes, old furniture and garbage bags from the house to the car in scorching August heat.

"*This* stuff is for Goodwill and *this* is for the dump," my mother orders, pointing for the umpteenth time to the piles she deliberately sorted. She begins poking through open boxes I had neatly packed, ready to be closed and labeled.

My irritation evident, I plead, "Please, *please*, Mom, those are done. We really need to work on the kitchen stuff."

"Och, I KNOW" my mother snaps. Throwing up her hands she turns her back to me and continues to rifle through the carefully organized items.

I whisper to Sharon, "What the hell?' My sister shrugs and bolts out the back door, cigarette lit before the door slams shut.

My mother faces me and in her signature staccato commands, "The attic. You. Must. Get. It. Done. Today."

I wonder—Had mom figured out that Sharon and I never actually went to Goodwill? That we decided instead to take everything to the dump? Was the attic my ultimate punishment? I stomp away. In an upstairs bedroom closet I yank open the narrow pull-down steps leading to the rafters of the house. Stifling heat envelopes me, cobwebs and dust swirl in slow motion above the cartons strewn about in the cramped space. Trip after trip I haul the attic contents down two flights of stairs, plopping each filthy box on the floor in the kitchen where my mother is haphazardly emptying cabinets and quite effectively, ignoring me.

I stumble on the bottom attic step spilling the contents of a box across the bedroom floor. In the mess is a large old-fashioned cookie tin. I open it and sift through the contents: odd buttons, a rusty broach and a wad of yellowed documents.

As I examine the papers it dawns on me that I am holding pieces of my mother's life. There are her travel documents from Belfast to America in 1956, arriving with two young daughters and reuniting with her husband after two- and-a-half-years apart. There are sad telegrams from Ireland—her mother died, then her brother died. There are old-fashioned savings passbooks, evidence of her endless struggles to save money, always, "robbing Peter to pay Paul," as she'd say. I find a crumpled letter dated January 1971 from a desperately poor, single, Jewish mother in our neighborhood. The woman thanks my mom for the food and toys she sent for the holidays. I can't help but chuckle. Leave it to my mom to make sure a couple of Jewish kids have a merry Christmas. There is an old payment booklet with neatly notated stubs in my mother's handwriting, all payments to the Singer Sewing Center; ten dollars a month for ten months, beginning in December 1973.

"Oh God." I whisper. That was the Christmas I begged incessantly for a Singer Genie sewing machine. A lot of the popular girls made their own clothes back then, even the captain of the cheerleading squad. From time I was in sixth grade I dreamed of being popular and at fifteen still stood on the outer rings of that exalted clique. I had believed that sewing machine was the answer to all my sophomoric prayers.

Back in the kitchen I put the kettle on for tea. Mom is asleep in a stuffed chair in the corner. I kneel down at her side and gently shake her awake.

"Attic's empty," I say, "What do you need me to do next?"

23

LAURA SHAINE CUNNINGHAM

Laura Shaine Cunningham is a novelist, memoirist, journalist, and playwright. She has published nine books. Her two memoirs, *Sleeping Arrangements* and *A Place in the Country*, were excerpted in *The New Yorker* and *The New York Times*. *A Place in the Country* was a *New York Times* Notable Book, and her fiction is printed in *The New Yorker, The Atlantic, Esquire,* and many literary journals. Laura's literary recognition includes two NEA awards, two NYFA awards, a Yaddo Fellowship, and a Ford Foundation award. Her play *Beautiful Bodies* is widely produced, and her play *Bang* was first produced by Steppenwolf Theatre. Her short plays are anthologized and performed in many festivals. She is currently nominated for a Pushcart Prize and published in *Monologues from the Edge*.

ON BEING MOTHERLESS

Laura Shaine Cunningham

When I read of children being orphaned, I feel the ache all over again. I lost my mother when I was eight years old and had never known my father.

One June morning, as I dressed for school, my mother showed me how to braid my hair in a special way that I liked. She was standing behind me at the vanity mirror, and I felt her hands tremble; her eyes met mine in the mirror.

"I should have shown you how to do this for yourself before..." she said. A catch in her voice alarmed me. Her eyes were overbright. I could see her bite her lower lip—I realized later; she was trying not to cry.

My mother told me that she had to go to a hospital, for routine tests, and when she returned home, we would have a holiday and go to the beach. She walked me to school as usual, and I waved goodbye through the fence. She was wearing a navy-blue blazer and skirt and high heels. She turned around once to have a look back at me.

I never really saw her again. I was not allowed into the hospital. A few days later, I caught a glimpse of my mother as I stood outside the hospital and saw her standing high above, in a tenth-floor window. She was wearing a pink nightgown. She had instructed me on the phone—"I am on the tenth floor—I will be at the fourth window from the left—You'll see me, in the pink silk..."

A few days later, the nightgown was folded in a box, in the apartment which we had shared, awaiting shipment to... to I know not where. Neighbors and relatives appeared at the small apartment where I had lived with my mother. Life, as I knew it, had ended—her death was sudden—only two weeks before, we had been on an excursion, and she had hiked with me and rowed a boat across Central Park Lake. Her death was incomprehensible to me. I remember hearing the word "orphan" and I could hardly believe that this word, so Dickensian, applied to me. The only orphans I knew of, were in literature—*A Little Princess* and *The Secret Garden* by Frances Hodgson Burnett, or in the comics—"Little Orphan Annie."

Would my life take on that grim Victorian plot? Might I be placed in an orphanage? Each dawn "after," I would wake up as if from a shuddering fall, knowing *something horrible has happened. How could I live without my mother?*

The box of my mother's clothes disappeared: her eye-glasses, her ice skates, her winter and summer clothes, her high heels and slippers—almost everything she had owned was packed up and given away. I hoarded what few items I could—bits of costume jewelry, an ivory heart-shaped pin, her perfume *Fleur de Lys*, an ice-skating sweater, and a special organdy "party" apron.

I still have the apron, tucked in my bureau drawer, and sometimes, I touch it, to remember. Even today, I sleep in a bedroom with my mother's portrait on the wall—I feel she watches over me, somehow.

Sometimes, on the street, I catch a glimpse of a woman, with dark curly hair, running, holding her wraparound swing coat closed, and I am tempted to catch up to her. A few weeks ago, I sat at a luncheonette counter, the kind of place my mother used to take me to have my favorite drink, a vanilla malted, and I looked up to see—my mother across from me. Before I realized it was only my own reflection on shining metal, I could swear—she smiled at me.

SADIE DINGFELDER

Sadie Dingfelder is a faceblind reporter, formerly of the *Washington Post*, now working on a book of funny personal essays.

MY IMAGINARY CHILDREN

Sadie Dingfelder

I have three musically gifted children. At least, that's what I told the lady sitting behind me at an orchestra performance I recently attended. I went with my friend and her three-year-old, and we were bopping along to the music in our seats. After a series of pointed huffs and sighs, a stern-looking woman tapped me on my shoulder. "Is that any way to teach a child how to behave at the symphony?" she said.

"It's a family concert," I replied.

"Well I have two children ..." she started to lecture.

"I have three, and they all play the cello," I countered.

That shut her up.

As it turns out, I don't have any kids at all. I used to explain my reasons. Now I just lie.

This all started when I was traveling in Indonesia, where asking about someone's kids is standard small talk, like mentioning the weather. Saying you don't have any—well, one cabdriver acted like I'd just told him I had terminal cancer.

"I'm so sorry," he said, his forehead creasing with concern.

"No, no it's fine," I said, trying to comfort him. "Look how much I get to travel."

The next person to ask was a man in a market.

"I have a daughter," I said. "She's eight."

"And you left her at home?"

He looked worried, and rightfully so. There I was, gallivanting around Asia while my little girl was a half-a-world away, scared and alone.

"She's with her grandparents," I said defensively. "She loves staying with them."

Since even pretend moms face the judgement of random strangers, I decided that my daughter should be a bit older.

"I just dropped her off at Smith College," I told another cabdriver, naming the school where I went because I couldn't think of any others on the fly. "We're so proud of her. She's all grown up," I added, tearing up a little.

"Just one daughter?" he said. "No sons?"

He was right. It was time to expand my family. For the rest of the trip, I had three kids, though their ages and genders varied. I borrowed names and details from my friends' progeny. Emma, seven, loves to swim and thinks she is a mermaid. Ethan, twelve, is having trouble paying attention in school.

"They want to put him on Ritalin, but I think he just has a lot of energy," I said. "Kids need to get outside and play, you know?" The man checking us out of the hotel nodded in agreement.

My boyfriend, characteristically silent during these exchanges, finally attempted to rein me in.

"It's time for you to settle down," he said, as we drove to the airport. "Pick a family and stick with it."

Back in America, I don't get to trot out my pretend children as often. But when I find myself at an elementary school talent show, for instance, they come in handy.

"Brent is such a good school, don't you think," said the woman next to me. "The teachers here are wonderful," I added, as if I had any idea.

I understand why people mistake me for a mom. I'm the right age, often in the right places, and my clothes are frequently covered in food stains. It helps that, having been to many baby showers, I've picked up the language.

"Sleep training is so hard," I told a new mother at a Christmas party last weekend.

"The baby Bjorn gives you more support, but the Ergo is so much easier to use," I later advised an expectant mom.

You may think being a pretend parent is the easy way out, but let me tell you, it's not. Between all the cello recitals and unicorn-riding lessons, I hardly know which way is up. Don't get me wrong, though. I wouldn't trade my imaginary children for anything in the world. Especially real ones.

This story first ran in the Washington Post's Solo-ish blog.

LYNN EDELSON

Lynn Edelson has studied memoir for years at the Writing Institute at Sarah Lawrence College, working with Kathy Curto and Steven Lewis. Though she refuses to indent her paragraphs, she is currently at work on a collection of short stories. In 2016 her essay, "Heart Monitor," was selected to be part of the New York City *Listen to Your Mother* show, and she's performed several of her pieces at Read650 live events. Lynn is the mother of two grown sons and works as a special educator and family trainer in the New York State Early Intervention Program. She lives in the Hudson Valley with her husband, Michael Principe, and two dogs who shed too much.

MOTHERING DAY

Lynn Edelson

Despite everything she couldn't do, and all the things she couldn't change, my mother was a remarkable woman. She was deaf in one ear, blind in one eye, stumbled too easily, but carried herself with dignity. She taught me how important it was to listen to the words that weren't said aloud, to stand up for those who could not, and to forgive.

"Find a less important place for your anger," she told me.

I was only forty-four when she died, too young to be without the one person who loved me, just because. After my father passed away, she began wandering the house in search of the man she loved. I longed for the mother I knew, the mother who didn't wear diapers, the mother who remembered my name.

Three days before she died, as she lay in a coma, my mother opened her eyes, looked into mine and whispered "I love you." I smiled, stroked her hand and kissed her finger-tips until she fell back asleep.

She never woke up again, and I thought my heart would break. I had been ready to let her go for months, until she came back to bid me farewell. And now I ached for my mother, the woman who loved me.

But then those other mommas stepped in, the women who loved her. And me. My Aunt Molly, my next-door neighbor Ruth, my cousin Phyllis. And all the GEHRIG AVENUE women who helped me cross the street when I was little, who gave me salami sandwiches and cookies and chocolate milk.

They took turns sitting with me on the driveway the day of the tag sale, the day strangers sifted through my parents' leftovers. Some sat quietly at my side, some entranced me with stories of the block and my childhood, but they all made sure that I ate, and that I was never alone.

And when it was finally time for me to go home, they hugged me tight as I bid farewell to my mother and the house I had grown up in. They were the elders who treasured her and me, the ones who reminded me that it all continues.

"Drive carefully and call me when you get there," Ruth said.

Then there are the sisters and friends who have gotten me through the challenges over the years. The ones who held my hand the first time the chemo flowed into my veins, the ones who jumped down into that hole to sit with me because they had been there and knew the way out. The ones who never faltered, who simply stood close and held me up when I could not stand. They gave me hope when I thought there was none. All of them mothers.

And the women in my life who have shown me different ways to turn the cube. Who give me the confidence to jump into the deep end of the pool, making me believe that anything is possible. They are the ones who listen to my written words; the ones who know that you can never eat too much chocolate or wear too much black. Mothers.

And the sons, also mothers, who cook for me and answer my texts day or night, reassuring me that I can in fact navigate my way through anything in this life, including the NYC subway system.

And my beautiful husband who mothers me too. On my darkest days he holds me close, dries my tears and reminds me that the sun is always shining behind the clouds.

So I've been thinking we should change the name of Mother's Day to Mothering Day. For those of us who have mothers who make us crazy, for those of us who have mothers who don't quite get it. For those of us whose mothers have left. And for those whose incredible mothers keep showing up when we need them.

JULIE EVANS

Julie Evans is a licensed massage therapist, ordained deacon, and freelance writer. Her writing has appeared on WebMD and in *Pulse, Healthy Hudson Valley,* and NPR's *The Roundtable.* Her essay "Sacred Touch" was published in the anthology *Into Sanity: Essays About Mental Health, Mental Illness, and Living In Between.* Julie holds advanced degrees in holistic health, pastoral counseling, mentoring theory, and narrative therapy. The author of *Joy Road: My Journey from Addiction to Recovery* (Woodstock Arts 2019), Julie lives in Woodstock, New York with her husband Tommy Porto and their cat, Marietta.

THE DOLL

Julie Evans

When I was seven my mom ran a program for adults with developmental disabilities that met at a convent. The nuns gave my mom a church pew to thank her. Ten years later my mom died and I inherited the pew. I don't know how I held onto it with all the crazy places my life took me. But at twenty-seven I bought a house and the little pew finally found its home.

The house I bought was old. I spent days sorting through the contents, loading the worst of it into a Buick that came with the deal. Fully loaded, I wound my way to the town dump. There was a pit for garbage surrounded by massive piles of junk. Behind a bonfire of brush and logs a mountain named Overlook stood guard. I emptied the Buick.

Marveling at the spectacle of hundreds of metal lawn chairs without their webbing I saw a big cloth doll stretched out on one of the broken chaise lounges. The doll was wearing a yellow jumpsuit with a purple scarf around her neck that looked like something my mother would wear. I ventured closer. I stood it up. It was a little shorter than me. The jumpsuit opened a bit and I saw a simple line drawing of a purple heart on its upper torso. I put the doll in the passenger seat and buckled her in.

Back at the house I put her on the pew in the mudroom and sat down next to her. As a little girl I'd sit on this pew watching my mom help the people in her program learn to do all sorts of things. She helped one lady learn how to talk and others how to cook or brush their teeth.

My mind was still on Mom as I got to work on organizing my new home. I cleaned and scrubbed the kitchen, took three doors off their hinges to open up the space, and as I hurried through the mudroom did a double take when I saw my mother sitting on the pew. My eyes flooded with tears.

It was the doll.

What was I going to do with her? I decided to put her in the garage and let that be that. Several hours later, though, I went out to the garage for a hammer and was startled as I pulled open the door and saw the doll. That was it. I loaded her in the Buick and headed back to the dump.

The dump was closed. With only a steel gate to keep cars out I figured I'd just carry her to her final resting place. I hid the car and unbuckled my charge from the passenger seat.

Carrying her in my arms to the gate I wedged both our bodies through a gap in the fence. Overlook Mountain loomed before me, the setting sun coloring the clouds a magnificent pink. It was then that I realized I had an opportunity to do something for my mom that I couldn't do at seventeen. I headed to the burn pit.

Walking toward the big logs crackling in the fire I wet my lips and looked around. I didn't see anyone. The doll became heavier with each step. I walked close enough to the fire to feel it tighten the skin on my face.

My mom had told my dad to cremate her if her time came first and he just couldn't. I hugged the doll to me. She became too heavy, the fire too hot; I threw her into the blazing pit. When the flames reached her arms for just the briefest moment I was sure I saw my mother's soft, beautiful hand raised in victory.

A sad happiness filled me as I returned home and sat down on the pew. Mama was free.

MARTHA FRANKEL

Martha Frankel is a writer, knitter, and research fanatic. She is the founder and executive director of Woodstock Bookfest, a yearly gathering of writers and readers, now in its eleventh year. On any given day, she'd rather be sitting on a porch, drinking coffee, talking to her mother.

REMEMBER

Martha Frankel

In every family photo taken before I'm fifteen, someone is holding my arms behind my back, as if I might float off if they weren't tethering me to the earth. Usually it was my mother, but in a few it was my sister Helene, and in one, my father.

We're looking at the photos now because my mother is going blind, and we want her to tell us who and what we don't recognize before it's too late.

"Everyone was always holding me back," I say.

"That's not true," my mother says. She gives each word the same emphasis. That's. Not. True.

My mother is staring into space, wearing dark sunglasses and smoking a Kent. Her gray hair stands out in little wisps. Her bottom lip is trembling. She looks like a pale Xerox of herself. Sylvia, yet not quite Sylvia.

The photos are spread on my sister's dining table. Helene sighs.

In my family I'm the drama queen. But when she starts to look through them she laughs. "Wow. I never noticed it before."

"Let me see," my mother demands.

She holds the photo close, but it's clear she can't make out details.

I take it back. "This one is at the bungalow colony. You've got me in some kind of wrestling lock!"

"What's everyone wearing?" my mother asks.

Helene grabs the photo. "I'm wearing madras shorts and a cardigan. I'm maybe thirteen. Martha's wearing those pedal pushers we couldn't get off her, and you have on..."

"Oh," my mother says dismissively. "Grandma took that photo. I have a babushka on my head, right? We were headed over to Monticello, to the racetrack. I can't imagine why I would have been holding Martha's arms."

I exchange a look with Helene; that was fifty years ago. My mother remembers where we were going? She's an elephant that way.

We look at another. "This was taken in front of Patricia Murphy's," Helene says. "You and I are holding Martha's wrists!" We're all quiet, remembering flaky popovers and salty, rare roast lamb; Patricia Murphy's was a warehouse-sized restaurant we went to celebrate something special. My mother's answer is a little click in the back of her throat.

I hold up another. In this one, it's clear our father was very sick, that cancer was ravaging his body. My sister and I gasp.

"What?" my mother asks, because she may be blind but her antennae are twenty/twenty.

"Daddy's sick," I say, suddenly listless.

"Where were we?" my mother asks.

I turn away. I don't like this game anymore.

"Miami," Helene whispers. "The San Souci hotel."

I was fifteen. I made out with a boy named Alan every day, at the pool, at the dances, in the staircase, wherever. My lips were chapped for weeks afterwards. I could recall the pattern of each garish shirt he wore, every single word he spoke to me between those kisses.

My father's sickness hadn't even registered. What kind of person am I?

My mother starts to laugh, a contagious, happy laugh that pulls Helene and me in, despite ourselves. That laugh grows in us.

"Remember how much fun daddy was?" my mother asks. "Remember he went to one of your dances, and he did the twist and the pony, and he was such a good dancer you weren't sure whether to be proud or embarrassed? Remember he taught you to drive when you were ten? Or how he would listen with all his attention, as if what you said was the most important thing in the world? Remember?"

For the first time in years I see my father not through the sorrow of his death, but through the shine of my mother's love.

"Remember?" she says again. That word, *remember*, makes us forget what it was we wanted to know. I put the photos back in the box and close the lid.

PAULA FUNG

Paula Fung lives in Rye, along with her husband, three daughters, and their dog, Boomer. She produces a show on public access television, *Rye Views* and writes personal essays on the things she knows, which are, in no particular order, cooking, sailing, and family life. Her work has been published on the *Sailing Anarchy* blog and Read650's *The Kids are Alright* and *Jew-ish*. She created and curates "Writes & Bites in Rye," a reading salon in her hometown of Rye, New York.

ROLE REVERSAL

Paula Fung

My daughter's hands were on my sweaty head, strong fingers making rhythmic circles deep into my damp scalp. She is an exercise instructor, teaching "Yoga Sculpt" and she's told me that during shavasana; the last posture, resting pose, she walks around and gives a gentle head massage to students as they lie on their backs, arms by their sides, palms up, in the dim light.

"Emily, that is not a normal thing to do. Why don't you go around and spray a light scent if you want to do something peaceful? Aren't there guys in your class?"

My husband and I had driven down to visit Emily at her home in Washington, DC. She graduated from Georgetown three years ago and took a job at a not-for-profit and fell in love with her yoga classes, which are called yoga, but are really based in heavy cardio.

"Leave early, so you can come to the class I'm teaching at five-thirty"

"Em, I am really not in shape for your classes."

"You can do it, other instructors' moms come!"

"I'm not sure, we're going to be tired from the drive."

"Mom-I'll get you in for free."

I never could resist a bargain.

"Ok, I'll try."

We get there, my husband checks us into the hotel, I change quickly into leggings, and Uber to the studio.

After a quick hug, Emily motioned me to the desk and said, "You're all checked in Paula! You can enter on the left, grab a towel and a mat!" Her hands hovered but didn't touch any computer keys, in case anyone was watching her "check me in"."

Lights are turned low and I'm glad.

No one would see my ratty toes desperately in need of a pedicure. I can't count the times I skipped yoga because I was embarrassed about my toes.

I sat cross-legged on the mat, and Emily began by saying, "You can dedicate this practice to whatever speaks to you. I've been thinking about grounding. I offer this for your dedication if it moves you as well."

It was a surreal experience to feel the thirty or so young men and women close their eyes and do as Emily says. I took a moment, hands to heart, to also dedicate my hour of yoga practice to "grounding" as it seemed as good a theory as any.

As we began, I squinted one eye open and observed Emily in her slim yoga pants and tiny exercise bra and wondered if all the yogis wore so little clothes, I couldn't picture them from other classes I'd taken. I marveled at her tuned abs and offered up a little prayer that her body doesn't eventually turn into mine, soft and generous, muscles deeply hidden. I once wore tiny bras too, until I breastfed three children and generally succumbed to the falling and flattening of time.

"Grounding" turned out to have been pretty ironic because suddenly there was lots of jumping and very little grounding. Her warriors did "bow and arrow" moves until my biceps and triceps wanted to cry. Her abdominal work consisted of Russian twists with high boat legs. I almost laughed when she yelled "jumping jacks!"

I hadn't done a jumping jack in decades. She quickly sequenced into "jumping jack, right cross-*punch,* jumping jack, left cross-*punch!*" I struggled to keep up, breathing heavily, feet barely leaving the floor on the jumps.

I didn't like having my child see me so markedly different from the majority of the class: struggling, winded, out of shape, vulnerable.

At shavasana, she came over and silently rubbed my head. Time stopped as I savored the strange sensation of my child's hands on me, she as the teacher, me as the student. Thankful again for the dark, my eyes filled with tears as part shame, part gratitude, and a good dose of pride all mingled with my sweat.

LISA GOLDSTEIN

Writer Lisa Goldstein is a Wall Street executive and recognized expert in healthcare finance. Her personal essays have been published annually in *Visible Ink Anthology* since 2015, three of which were selected for staging at the *Visible Ink* performances in New York City. Lisa's essay, "Goal! Telling my 10-Year Old about my Diagnosis" was published on breastcancer.org and Women You Should Know published her essay "To Dye or Not to Dye." In 2015, Lisa was selected to read her humorous essay, "Summer of George," at the northern New Jersey edition production of *Listen to Your Mother*. Lisa lives in Manhattan with her husband and two teenagers. She writes when she's not analyzing income statements or helicopter parenting.

FEARLESS GIRL MEETS FEARLESS GIRL
Lisa Goldstein

I was running behind when I came out of the subway, racing home to scoop up my daughter and travel across town to a doctor's appointment. But a construction worker had commandeered the sidewalk with his survey equipment, forcing me to slow down and walk around him.

Annoyed, I rhetorically asked him what he was doing. I got an impromptu engineering lesson back. He pointed to another crew member across the street holding a prism. "The prism creates an unbroken line from the sidewalk to the new building. That's how we know it will be perfectly straight."

"Perfectly straight." That caught me off guard. I hoped it was a good sign: that afternoon Julie and I were going to see an orthopedist about the curve in her spine.

Julie's scoliosis diagnosis resonated hard with me. When I was her age I wore a hot, thick plastic brace for two long years. All day, every day. To straighten out the curve of my curve.

It was awful.

49

It wouldn't be until well after those two years that I realized it wasn't that bad. But of all the curveballs life could throw my daughter, why did curvature of the spine have to be one of them?

I told my nervous thirteen-year-old daughter that she could handle this. I called her my fearless girl, like the statue in lower Manhattan. *Fearless Girl* stood defiantly, staring down *Charging Bull*. She could take on anything.

Today I needed to be fearless. I needed to walk into that appointment defiant, chest out, back... kinda' straight, hands placed squarely on my uneven hips, ready to take on scoliosis again, this time for my daughter. But when we arrived, I melted. I was fearful.

The waiting room was crowded. There were kids in wheelchairs, others with permanent braces on their legs. I wondered if Julie noticed.

A nurse escorted us to the exam room and measured her height with a stadiometer, informing us that it took months for the engineers to install it. "We had to make sure the floor was one hundred percent level so the scale would be perfectly straight."

There were those words again.

The doctor walked in, examined Julie's back and gave us her expert thoughts: "The curve is subtle; there's likely no need to do anything. Let's take an x-ray to make sure."

We floated down the hall to imaging and then back again, my now weightless daughter gliding on my unencumbered back. A few minutes later the doctor came in and swiveled the computer screen so we could all see.

Click.

The shadowy x-ray appeared instantly, and one thing was clear: that curve was NOT subtle. It looked like someone yanked a thick chain, hard. "Oh." The doctor's voice dropped a few decibels. "Not what I thought."

The room grew quiet. Then a tsunami hit.

The doctor wanted to brace her right away. Could we come back tomorrow for measurements and a fitting?

I looked at my daughter, her blue eyes now rimmed in watery red. I found my fearless voice and informed the doctor that Julie was leaving for camp in a few days. Unless two months would make a difference, we would revisit this later, when she got home. From camp.

We walked out in silence. It was my daughter who spoke up first.

"There were so many disabled kids in that waiting room, Mom," she whispered. "Maybe a brace won't be so bad...."

She had gained a lifetime of perspective in one afternoon. My fearless girl was indeed my *Fearless Girl*. Whatever she faced she could handle.

"You can do this!" I assured her, wrapping my arms around her. "We'll deal with this when you get home from camp."

A small smile came across her face.

My daughter's spine may have been curved, but I knew her head was on straight.

Perfectly straight.

CATHERINE HILLER

Catherine Hiller is the author of *Just Say Yes: A Marijuana Memoir* and *Skin: Sensual Tales*, about which John Updike wrote, "Good, brave, and joyful writing." Among her other publications are several short stories in *Penthouse*, five novels, two pieces in the *New York Times Sunday Review*, and a feature in *AARP Magazine*. She has a PhD in English from Brown University, and her most recent novel is *The Feud* (2018) about a deadly workplace rivalry.

ALL I ASK

Catherine Hiller

We are in the kayak, my mother and I, and although the water is calm and we're both wearing life jackets, I'm having second thoughts. After all, we're a great distance from shore, too far to swim back, and my mother is ninety years old. She had a little trouble getting into the kayak: what if it overturns? Could she push her way out and bob to the top?

I've been paddling for many years and haven't capsized a kayak yet, and the bay is smooth. "This is so lovely," she says. "I feel so safe with you."

It's the best thing she could have said, and I stop worrying.

"Let's go to Shelter Island!"

"Mom, that's much too far. And the current's too strong."

We paddle across the bay toward the point.

I start to breathe in synch with my strokes: two strokes when I inhale, four when I exhale. This feels very good: my breath, my body, and the boat now feel aligned.

In back of me, my mother has stopped paddling and is singing a song in French, off key. She has a greater capacity for joy than anyone I know.

When we reach the point, I let the kayak drift and rest my fingers in the water, which feels warmer than the air.

As we return, mother chants in my ear, "I must go down to the seas again, down to the.. . how does it go?"

I remember the first verse of the John Masefield poem, "Sea Fever," and turn so she can hear me:

> I must go down to the sea again,
> To the lonely sea and sky
> And all I need is a tall ship
> And a star to steer her by.

We make a smooth landing on the beach. I disembark, pull the kayak higher, and carefully help my mother out, at one point bearing her weight, which is all of ninety pounds.

Once home, I run to her computer and quickly find the Masefield poem. Suddenly, my eyes are wet. My mother would be so pleased if she could see my tears. But no, that would be cheap; I will not let myself cry when I read her the poem. That's all I ask: not a single tear.

I say, "Here are the words to the poem." I start to read. I get through the first verse okay. Then I start on the second. By "a wild call and a clear call," my eyes have started to fill; by "all I ask," my voice is a croak, and by "sea-gulls," I'm crying right along with them.

My mother is thrilled. "I'm so glad I have a daughter who can respond so deeply to literature."

I shake my head and find myself saying, "No, no, this is dishonest." I take a deep shuddering breath and make it almost to the end of the last stanza before breaking down again.

And all I ask is a merry yarn from a laughing fellow-rover,
And quiet sleep and a sweet dream when the long trick's over.

Snot is flowing down my nose: I'm sobbing. I've suddenly seen that the poem is about life itself; death is the quiet sleep, and because we must die, life is a trick, both in the nautical meaning of "tour of duty" and in the common meaning of "cheat."

I want my gallant little mother to live forever – that's all I ask.

"What do you mean by dishonest?" she says.

I shake my head; it's too complicated to explain. For I'm sure that in wanting to please her, I somehow manufactured those forbidden tears.

"Why did you say dishonest?" she insists.

"Why don't you figure it out?"

Her face is keen, she is up for the challenge, she wants to kayak to Shelter Island. She asks, "Will you tell me if I'm right?"

MARIE PROELLER HUESTON

Author and illustrator Marie Proeller Hueston has written for *Country Living, Town & Country, Milieu,* and *Art & Auction.* Her children's books include *The All-American Jump and Jive Jig* and *Christmas Eve with Mrs. Claus.* A contributor to Nickelodeon's former parenting humor site, *NickMom,* she is currently working on a book of her "mom comics" about the funny and frustrating aspects of parenting. Her essay "The Outsiders" was part of Read650's *Tales of New York.*

NEVER LET THEM SEE YOU JUMP
Marie Proeller Hueston

It happened one afternoon, quite by accident: My children discovered that I startle easily. I was coming out of our downstairs bathroom when my daughter, six-years-old at the time and for some reason idling beneath a kitchen stool, innocently greeted me.

"Hi, Mom!"

Not expecting to hear a voice at floor level, I sprang into the air and let out a yelp.

You'd think that she'd stumbled upon a cache of birthday presents, the way she squealed with delight at her unintended "gotcha" moment. She wriggled out from under the stool and raced upstairs to tell her big brother what had happened.

After that, my days became a unique kind of hell. Around every corner, a small child lurked.

"Hi, Mom!" they'd chirp, eyes aglow in the hopes of frightening me again.

"You got me!" I'd reply, pretending to be amused but secretly wondering how long it would take for the novelty to wear off.

"Remember when you were coming out of the bathroom and you screamed and jumped up in the air?" they'd remind me with each new attempt.

"Yes! Very funny! You really got me that time!"

Their let's-scare-mom scheme reached its peak one night around bedtime. Both children were occupied, my son finishing up his reading homework and my daughter coloring in her room. I naïvely thought I could sneak in a quick shower without anyone noticing. There, in the warm and relaxing steam, I let down my guard. It was the first time in weeks I wasn't steeled against the next ambush.

As I turned off the water and slid open the shower door, my son stood before me with a mischievous grin on his face.

"Hi, Mom!" he piped.

"THAT IS NOT FUNNY!" I screeched, my moment of serenity vanquished in an instant. "I DO NOT LIKE IT WHEN

YOU DO THAT! STOP SCARING ME!"

His surprised and slightly apprehensive expression at the sight of me — naked, dripping wet, and fuming — brought me back to myself. I dialed it down (and grabbed a towel), explaining that pranks can sometimes be taken too far. He seemed to absorb what I was saying and, with a shrug of his shoulders, went back to reading. He'd seen me freak out before.

I often wonder which vision of their mother my children will carry with them into adulthood. Will it be the person who went along with the joke ninety-nine percent of the time or the one who occasionally lost her cool? Fortunately for me, history tends to be kind to parents who try their best.

LUCILLE ISCARO

Lucy Iscaro has always been a writer but only recently; since retiring from full-time teaching and part-time tutoring, she has she been able to devote herself to the craft. Her essays have appeared in print in the *New York Times, Good Old Days Magazine,* and *Reflections.* On-line essays have appeared on boomercafe.com and Read650.org and the 2019 edition of Word Fountain contains some of her poetry. She shares her White Plains, New York home with her husband and dog who both encourage and inspire her work. For the past few years she has been part of a supportive community of writers in workshops led by novelist Barbara Josselsohn and poet Carmen Mason.

LEORA

Lucille Iscaro

My first grandchild had blond hair and blue eyes, and resembled no one else in the family. This had less to do with genetics than with the fact that she was a doll.

I had told my daughters that fads and trends were to be resisted. Still, in the early 1980's, when my youngest daughter, Jennifer, admired a friend's Cabbage Patch Kid I was touched by the longing in her eyes. But it was nearly Christmas and the stores were out of the enormously popular toy.

"Listen Honey," I told her, "I waited nine months to get you. You're going to have to wait too."

Chanukah came and went. Barbie got her Dream House but Jen didn't get her dream doll. Even though she was happy with her new toys she still yearned for that kid.

This was a difficult holiday season for my girls and me. Their dad had moved out in the fall and we were feeling our way around this new territory. I told them over and over that we were still a family, just a different kind of family. But it was hard to ignore the empty seat at the dinner table, the missing car in the driveway, or the gap in the closet. One less goodnight kiss spoke louder than any of my reassurances. That elusive toy became Ahab's white whale for me. My little girl needed this doll and I needed to get it for her.

In those pre-Internet days, you either had to haunt the stores daily to find the toy of the moment or you had to know someone. My neighbor, whose daughter had also caught the Cabbage Patch fever, had gotten an inside tip that there was a new shipment at Macy's. We had to be fast. Like a suburban mom version of a heist movie we went in a back door and hustled our prizes out fast.

The doll came with official papers proclaiming we had adopted one Leora Carlotta. We, her new family, were cautioned to never refer to her as a doll. She was a baby and my freckle-faced daughter was her mom. I, by extension, was Grandma.

Jennifer quickly ripped open the cardboard box and lovingly stroked the curly yarn hair. In minutes the old baby clothes I'd stored in the attic were repurposed. Our already hectic morning routine had a new step. Leora had to be stripped of her pajamas and dressed in an outfit that coordinated with her mom's. After breakfast Jen would sit her baby on the couch near the front window to await their after-school reunion.

She was not a doll that did any tricks. Unlike more realistic dolls she didn't eat, poop, or speak. She did just one thing and she did it very, very, well. She would lie still and compliant while my daughter held her, hugged her, and told her about her day. For that I was grateful.

One cold night my girls went out with their dad leaving me in a house that had minutes ago been too noisy and was now painfully quiet. I had been entrusted with my granddaughter's care and I went to change her into pajamas. When I lifted her a scent of baby lotion floated up from under her dress and I was engulfed by a wave of nostalgia. I knew that the aroma was synthetic and yet I shifted Leora into a more comfortable position in my arms. It was just as I had held my babies in the years before, when they were small and I could give them all they needed. I cradled and hugged her and told her about my day. She was still and compliant and I was grateful.

SALLY KOSLOW

Sally Koslow, the former editor-in-chief of *McCall's* magazine, is the author of six books translated into fourteen languages. Her latest work is *Another Side of Paradise*, a biographical novel about F. Scott Fitzgerald's Hollywood love affair with Sheilah Graham, a movie industry reporter who exposed the secrets of others while hiding secrets of her own. Sally contributes essays to magazines, newspapers, anthologies and websites, including the *New York Times, Oxford University Press, Real Simple, O, the Oprah Magazine, More* and many others. She has spoken at the F. Scott Fitzgerald Society in France, colleges, libraries, women's clubs, synagogues and Generation Women, a female storytelling night in New York City, and has taught creative writing privately and at The Writing Institute at Sarah Lawrence College. www.SallyKoslow.com

ADD ONE TEASPOON
OF MOTHER LOVE

Sally Koslow

In my childhood, women baked in self-defense. If Fargo,
North Dakota, had any bakeries, they must have been hidden
in underground silos. If you wanted a decent dessert, you
drove 221 miles north to Winnipeg, drove 235 miles southeast
to Minneapolis. or greased a pan and pre-heated the oven to
350 degrees. Sensible women chose the latter.

Until my mother detoured into Bundt-land, her default
recipe featured instant pudding, vodka, and Galliano—she
prepared treats every Friday: pies; prune bread (sounds vile,
tasted heavenly), a parade of cookies, bars, and a blizzard
of cakes–airy angel food, heart-shaped layers for Valentine's
Day, and sheet cakes crowned with broiled coconut or her
mother's seven-minute frosting. When I went off to college,

Mom shipped me butterscotch oatmeal cookies in coffee cans.
I suspect my boyfriend—now, husband—stuck around mostly
because he had a crush on the cookies.

My mother never considered her baking special, so neither did I, and I spent my adolescence longing for a mom who
could butter my ego while sharing wisdom to help me become
irresistible to boys and enviably chic. I wanted Coco-Chanel-
meets-Jackie-O. What I got was a life member of Hadassah in
anklets and orthopedic wedges whose hair flair flatlined at
pin curls and who, at the first rumble of stress, crashed with
a four-day migraine. I yearned for a storybook relationship
past the time I, too, became a mom. Then, abruptly, the fantasy
imploded. I took my mother to a concert at the Metropolitan
Museum, which she insisted was the University of Minnesota,
where she'd gone to college. I didn't need a diagnosis of dementia—that came the next year—to guess what was happen-
ing, although Mom was barely sixty. For the next few weeks, I
couldn't staunch my tears—for her tragedy and to be honest,
for mine: the bond I dreamed of, measured by the high stan-
dards of my imagination, was never going to happen.

Soon, my mother forgot who I was. When we visited the
nursing home where she now lived, disquietly decorated with
residents' childlike artwork, my husband and I tried to pene-
trate the maximum-security prison that is dementia. "Do you
remember the recipe for those cookies you sent Sally at col-

lege?" he asked one afternoon. Recognition twinkled. "I forgot that recipe a long time ago," my mom joked. It was the last coherent sentence I ever heard her utter.

Two years after my mother's death, I had a dream. She was preparing Thanksgiving dinner and for dessert, she'd baked pumpkin pie, for which she gave me pointers: "Plain whipped cream has no flavor. Always add vanilla and confectioners' sugar." As she showed me the amounts, her voice was strong and her demeanor, alive. I woke with a smile. The dream was both hello and good-bye.

When a friend has a dinner party, I'm the one who always volunteers to bring dessert. As I bake, often from recipes in my mom's handwriting, I hear her Marge accent that I left in Fargo. "Refrigerate the dough." "Don't make a crust if the kitchen's muggy." "Take the eggs out early to get to room temperature." "Measure accurately–baking depends on chemical reactions." "Always wash the top of a can—it may be dusty." I'm back in our childhood kitchen. Outside, sun bounces off snowdrifts, but inside, it's cozy, warmed by the legacy of my mother's love.

ANN LEVIN

Ann Levin is a writer and editor. A longtime journalist, she was national news editor of the *Associated Press*, where she worked for twenty years. Before that she was a reporter for the *San Diego Tribune* and other newspapers. She has also written for *USA Today*, *AARP*, *The Forward*, *Sensitive Skin*, *Meat for Tea*, and other publications. She lives in New York City and is currently working on a memoir. Learn more at www.AnnElizabethLevin.com

THE BEST STUDENT

Ann Levin

My mother took up Pilates in the last fifteen years of her life, when her hands were too arthritic to grip a tennis racket. She loved her teacher so much, my siblings and I invited her to speak at Ma's memorial. As Sharon stepped up to the podium, I recalled all the times Ma had told me, "Oh my God, she's so beautiful!" And she was, with a dancer's lithe body and shiny dark hair.

Ma worshipped physical beauty. It's one of the million things we fought about. But she had her reasons. She grew up thinking she was ugly, which she wasn't. She just had the misfortune of being born in 1926—thirty years before ethnic looks were in, a Barbra Streisand in a Marilyn Monroe kind of world.

Her parents had died of cancer when she was a little girl, and she was sent to live with her Aunt Kate, a large, forbidding character straight out of *Jane Eyre*. Kate once told her,

"Sally, you might not be pretty, but you're smart." As a result, all Ma cared about was being pretty.

She longed to look like the movie stars of the 40s—high cheekbones, smooth hair, tiny, upturned nose. I came of age in the 60s and adored Janis Joplin, her hippie rags and wild hair. After 1968, when I was a freshman in high school, I quit wearing makeup, threw away my curlers, and spent the next fifty years in ratty T-shirts and ripped jeans.

Whenever I went to visit Ma in Pittsburgh, she'd beg me to take a lesson with Sharon, using her signature mix of persuasion and humiliation. "It will help your posture, hon," she'd say. "It's so important as we age."

I went once or twice, reluctantly, because Pilates is hard. The studio is a cross between a physical therapy clinic and a medieval torture chamber, with sliding platforms and tables fitted out with leather straps, springs, pulleys, and stirrups.

The worst exercise is called The Hundreds. You lie on your back, raise your legs at an angle, and pump your arms up and down, panting maniacally like a woman in labor. The only thing holding up the massive levers of your legs are the muscles of your core—and sadly, mine just weren't as strong as my aging mother's.

To her, it was catnip. All her life she'd operated at a frightening level of physical intensity: five kids in eight years, a big house and garden, schlepping boxes and moving sofas in the family furniture store. She played hard too—tennis, skiing, step aerobics, yoga. She had toned upper arms long before Michelle Obama made it cool.

In her eulogy Sharon talked about how Ma was always the best student, able to do exercises in her 70s that most women in their 30s would struggle to complete. Toward the end, after Ma was diagnosed with cancer, they focused on the theme, "Resistance makes you stronger." It was a notion she knew well, after being orphaned at five, widowed at sixty-two, and losing a son—my older brother—when he was only forty.

When my sisters and I were cleaning out her drawers, I took home twelve pairs of her Pilates socks and started to go to a studio around the corner. It's been five years since she died, three months shy of her eighty-ninth birthday, and I'm still at it.

I've even found my Sharon, only her name is Allegra. She's beautiful too, with a dancer's lithe body and shiny brown hair. Whenever she gives me some horrific exercise to perform, I do what I think Ma would have done—dig down deep and gut it out. I still don't love it as much as she did, but whenever I leave the studio, I walk a little taller, and a few people have even told me that my posture has gotten better.

BETTY MacDONALD

Writer/performer Betty MacDonald contributed and performed in TMI's *What to Expect When You're Not Expecting* at Woodstock's Bearsville Theatre. Her essays and poems are included in the anthologies *Get Out of My Crotch!*, *80 Things to Do When You Turn 80*, *Better with Age* and *Open House*. Betty has been a featured reader at Spoken Word in Kingston, New York, Read650 at the Cell Theatre in New York City, and The Best of Read650 at Vassar College. In October 2019, she interpreted six roles for Work Project at Catskill's Bridge Street Theatre. For thirty years Betty has honed her storytelling abilities as an active cast member with Community Playback Theater in the Hudson Valley. She reads frequently at Words Carry Us, a monthly series she hosts at Green Kill in Kingston, New York.

DAUGHTER OF TWINS

Betty MacDonald

I am the daughter of twins. Doris gave me life and raised me. Minerva her twin sister adopted me many years after my mother died when I was sixty-three. Minerva was ninety-one.

The twins identified strongly with each other their whole lives even dressed alike well into their teens. They didn't look alike or sound alike, but they said a lot of the same things. Because Doris was the more mellow of the two, when Minerva spoke, it was like having an actor with a bad attitude read my mom's lines.

Doris married first and had a baby, my brother Sam. Then Minerva married and gave birth to David. The score was even, but not for long. When the doctor told Minerva she couldn't have more children, she became resentful, not toward my mother for out-birthing her with a daughter, but toward me for being that daughter. She never liked me.

The feeling was mutual.

A few weeks after my mother died at age seventy-nine, Minerva's fifty-three-year-old son was dead of a stroke. With the loss of the two most important people in her life, my aunt was crushed. I was grieving as well but concerned that with the death of her son Minerva had no reach into the future. It was clear that without my help she would be utterly alone. I set aside my bad feelings and become Minerva's caretaker. For over a decade I traveled regularly from my home in the Hudson Valley to attend to her in Northern New Jersey.

Twelve years later out of the blue Minerva called to tell me she wanted to adopt me. I was to meet her and Alan, her lawyer at the courthouse in Hackensack. When I asked why, she said, "It's Alan's idea," as if that was explanation enough.

In yet another attempt to please my cantankerous aunt, and with my lawyer's advice that I had nothing to lose, I agreed to the adoption. After all, I had already taken on the duties of a flesh and blood daughter and with my new status, I was insured access to her if in failing health, she were hospitalized.

The adoption was straightforward and unsentimental. The formalities concise and the judge cordial. As we left the judge's chambers, Alan, by way of celebration said to Minerva, "Now you have a daughter!" As negative as ever, Minerva replied, "but she won't listen to me." She never divulged what it was I wasn't listening to, or for that matter, the reason for the adoption.

Admirably active into her nineties, Minerva swam at the Y and continued to drive until she made an unfortunate left turn into oncoming traffic, totaling her car and her confidence. After that, I drove her everywhere she needed to go.

One day when I arrived, she excitedly showed me a silky shawl she had painstakingly adorned with long fringe that floated gracefully as she pretended to twirl around the room. The gift of creativity had momentarily awakened in her a long-dormant girlish glee. It was a privilege for me to glimpse what had been.

Minerva was an unusual combination of generosity and meanness. She replaced my car when it broke down and propped up my finances when my freelance work hit a lull. At the same time, she continued to find fault with me. Only once near the end of her life did she say, "I don't know how I would manage without you!" Unaccustomed to praise from her, I gratefully thanked her. "Well," she said, "If I'd known it meant so much to you, I would have told you sooner." She never mentioned it again.

Minerva died in her ninety-fifth year on Valentine's Day on the second day of the first vacation I'd taken in years. I flew back from Florida and made arrangements for my adopted mother.

KATHRYN MAYER

Kathryn Mayer—known as Kathy and Kate—is a potty-mouth writer, humorist, and activist writing out loud with humor and angst about social issues, parenting, midlife, and gun violence prevention at kathrynmayer.com. She is occasionally funny on Instagram and Twitter @ kathykatemayer and plays well with others on Facebook. She's a reluctant inductee into AARP, mom of four mostly grown-and-flown kids, and an aspiring writer with rejections to prove it. Her blog is a National Society of Newspaper Columnist award winner, received the Connecticut Press Club award for Best Personal Blog in Connecticut, and has received BlogHer Voice of the Year honors. Her essays appear online, in print, and most often on fridges, sticky with smiles and swears.

REMOTE CONTROL

Kathryn Mayer

My mother's television remote is broken and somehow this is my fault.

She calls, often, to let me know. As if I could ever forget.

My mother is not an invalid. She is not helpless, far from it. She is also not the stereotypical made-for-TV, warm-and-cozy, milk-and-cookies grandmotherly type. Not a chance.

She's more Grandma 2.0, a tech-savvy senior first in line at Apple for the latest and greatest i-whatever. Sure, she's a crazy cat lady who quilts, reads, and does yoga, yet she is also on Instagram, Facebook and, my kids assure me, Snapchat.

She has one Facebook account for her iPad, another for her iPhone, because who has time to remember all these passwords, Kathy. If she had more electronics, she'd have more Facebook profiles, you can bet on it.

She is not a wallflower, but instead a brick wall. Of opinion. Of attitude. Of brains, strength, will power, and conviction. She's politically active, loud, opinionated, and not a fan of waiting her turn. Ever.

She can convince, convert and complain effectively enough to get cable companies to show up, doctors to give personal cell numbers, and credit card companies to refund late fees and ——get this——apologize.

And yet, if something breaks in her home, this is my fault. Mine. The six degrees of separation knows no limits.

"Kathy? Are you there? This is YOUR MOTH-ER," she shouts each syllable with deliberate enunciation into voicemail. *"T-V re-mote NOT work-ing. RE-MOTE. BRO-KEN. You fixed hot water heater, now remote does NOT work. AT ALL."*

Click.

Water heater. Remote.. I don't see the connection, but okay.

"Kath-y? Is that you? It is YOUR mother. NO POW-ER. Power is OUT. Using cell phone. POWER OUT. You fixed printer, and now POWER IS OUT."

Click.

For someone so tech savvy, she has yet to grasp the ins and outs of the telephone and is always surprised if I actually answer the phone.

"Kathy? Is that you?"

Yes mom. You called me. On my cell. It's me.

"Oh, didn't sound like you. The garage door, it's not opening. And yes, I pushed the button. It's broken, ever since you were here to help with the cats. What did you do? Hasn't worked the same since. Kathy? Are you there?"

Yes mom. I'm here.

She's equally surprised when her calls are somehow sent to voicemail, which happens. A lot. Because Caller ID and all.

"Kath-y? Dry-er BRO-KEN. BRO-KEN. Does not work. Loud noise. Wi-fi working, but dryer broken. Call me back. This is your mother."

Click.

"Kath-y? Net-flix. Not work-ing. Log-in. Fail. This is your mother."

Click.

She leaves messages as if English were not my first language.

As if I had another mother.

Despite living several area codes away, and regardless of her innate talent to navigate the internet and customer service with ease and remarkable success, it is me she calls first with whatever crisis besieges her.

So, I respond with my own midlife teenage temper tantrum, ignoring incessant texts and sending calls to voicemail. I claim Facebook abstinence to relentless posts and messages. I tattle desperately to my sisters and beg one of them to take the fall—I mean, the call.

But I remain a good daughter, so eventually, in a couple hours, or maybe days, I do call back.

Sorry, Mom, missed your call. I'm working. What's up?

And it begins, her long list of grievances, calling to attention all that is not working in her life.

Here's the thing: she is me. She is my future; I can feel it coming.

Someday, sooner than I care to admit, my own TV remote will die, and I without fail will text a kid or two, maybe leave a staccato, desperate voicemail about malfunctioning life, and ramble on about how I need them to listen, please, and come right away to fix whatever is broken.

MARSHALL MESSER

Marshall Messer has recently retired from teaching high school English and is trying to figure out what to do with his life. He has been a cab driver, bartender, garbageman, actor, and he has played blues harp at the Rock and Roll Hall of Fame. He is the author of the novel *Change at Jamaica.*

MY MOTHER:
THE UNAUTHORIZED BIOGRAPHY

Marshall Messer

My mother never just walked into a room—she always made an entrance. Soon Bette would be rattling off a steady stream of witty lines and off-color jokes: "You know I have three children who are three different sexes—a boy, a girl, and a *vonce.*" *Vonce,* if you don't know, is Yiddish for bedbug, to my little sister's everlasting chagrin. "Have I showed you the three-carat ring my husband bought me? He loves me very much!" Her finger displayed a novelty gewgaw with three plastic orange carrots. Then she'd remove a square of colored paper from her handbag, start folding, and in seconds a frog or crane would take shape, which she'd gift away to members of her rapt audience. Or she'd perform this parlor trick that would appear to elongate her thumb by a couple of inches: "But first you have to say the magic words: *abracadabra, presto change-o, ala kazam!*" Adults were charmed; four-year-olds were in awe. On leaving, she'd announce to the lucky object of her attentions, "You have uplifted my spirit and enriched my soul."

As Bette would say: "The poor bastards never knew what hit 'em."

My mother had a saying for every occasion. While putting on makeup, she'd invariably remark, "Powder and paint can make you what you ain't." When we criticized her, she quipped, "It's very hard bringing up parents nowadays." As we left for school in the morning, she'd remind us to "walk between the raindrops." I swear, she could've had a career with Hallmark.

As the years passed, Bette repeated herself so often that to her teenaged children her shtick became stale and predictable. What people she met for the first time saw as amusing, I took as a cue to roll my eyes. Oh, she was still endlessly entertaining, so long as you weren't her child.

Yeah, she was a character, my mother. And because I was too close to her, it took me longer to appreciate her special talents.

A first-generation American, Bette was nine months old when she arrived with her parents at Ellis Island. Her first language was Yiddish, and her life in Bensonhurst was marked indelibly by the hardscrabble realities of the Depression. Yet she persevered, she dreamed, she assimilated. She graduated City College, worked as a bookkeeper, married an ambitious man, and moved out of gritty Brooklyn to raise her family in the suburbs.

I was in college when my father died suddenly of a heart attack. Bette was in shock, as we all were. The day of the funeral, a letter arrived informing me that I had been expelled for violating university policy, having flunked a course in both the fall and spring semesters. "Oy, Marshall, I need this like a hole in the head." But, as the terra firma of college life liquified beneath my feet, Bette sprang into action. She phoned the dean and assured him that, overnight, I had become keenly aware of my responsibilities. She looked at me. "I think it's fair to say, Dean Dietrich, that his father's death has slapped Marshall hard across the face,"—she mimed giving me the back of her hand—"and now he's fully awake. If you give him another chance, I know he'll make the most of it." Her voice brimmed with heightened emotion. "She hung up and said, "Where's my Academy Award?" A week later, Cornell gave me a second chance.

According to Japanese legend, cranes live to be a thousand years old. They say if you fold a thousand paper cranes, you will live to a ripe old age. Thanks, no doubt, to all that origami, Bette lived to be eighty-four.

When she died, my sisters and I wrote down her favorite sayings searching for what to put on her headstone. The phrase we chose was Bette to a T: "Never a dull moment."

MARGARITA MEYENDORFF

Margarita Meyendorff is the author of the published memoir *DP: Displaced Person*. The daughter of a Russian baron, she was born displaced in a refugee camp in Germany, far from the opulence of Imperial Russia that was her birthright. She has performed as an actress, dancer, musician, and storyteller at venues throughout the United States and in Europe. Her memoir is being translated in Russian for publication in Russia next year, and Margarita's short stories have been published internationally; one of her stories, "Rudolf Nureyev," recently won the New Millennium Writing Award. Margarita is currently working on an anthology of short stories based on her numerous life adventures entitled *Flipping the Bird*.

RENDEZVOUS

Margarita Meyendorff

Was it a dream? A hallucination? Psychic manifestation? I don't know. I know it happened and it seemed as real as this present moment.

It was early spring. It could have been Paris, or Morocco, or Martinique—anywhere French. It had to be French. A hopeless romantic, she loved places French.

I chose Paris. A café in the St. Montmartre district. I arrived first brimming with anticipation—I had waited a long time for this encounter. To calm myself, I ordered a glass of chilled rosé and a shot of cold Stolichnaya vodka for her and I waited; my mind filled with our past. Why can't I recall what she called me in my childhood? Mourka? Mourik? Never Mourechka, the most endearing...Did I ever take her to a nice restaurant where she could be pampered and spoiled with delicious food and drink? Never. Tonight, I will lavish and spoil her with a high-end delicious French dinner, the best wine, the best vodka...*Will she be angry? Affectionate? Will we have enough make-up time?*

I noticed her when she first appeared at the entrance of the café. She stood and waited for the *maître d'* to show her to our table. She had on an unremarkable grey coat and a grey *chapeau* that covered her grey hair. She was never very tall; her shoulders drooped a little more now and she clutched her pocketbook as she searched the café for a familiar face.

I beckoned her to our table. I stood up as she came toward me. We stared at each other not knowing exactly what to say, then we embraced. The embrace was awkward as there weren't too many embraces back then.

She took off her coat and hat and sat down, lit a cigarette and looked at me as if to say, *why did you bring me here?* She was as I remembered her. She was dressed in a white blouse and black skirt below her knees—simple but still elegant. Her grey thick wavy hair was pulled back with brown plastic combs and her pale oval face was covered with wrinkles. I saw that she made an effort and applied some mascara and put on red lipstick, but she could never hide that perpetual sadness which permeated her entire being. Even when she was young and beautiful and her skin soft and unmarked, she had that sad far-away look.

She looked beautiful to me.

The last time I saw her, she was in an alcoholic daze trying to focus on a bridge game with my father, my future husband

and me. In her eyes, I was getting married and doing the right thing for the first time in my life. I knew I was losing my soul. Five years later, I was living in Minneapolis with my husband and two-year-old daughter when my mother fell on the floor with a cigarette in one hand and a shot of vodka in the other. A week later, she died of a massive stroke.

I broke the silence.

"Мама," I said in Russian, the language we shared, "Можем ли мы начать всё сначала?" "*Can we start over?*"

She put out her cigarette, swallowed the shot of vodka then took my hands in hers.

"Можем." "*We can.*"

We held hands and looked at each other. This was not an apparition. It was Mama. I saw tears well up in her eyes and start to run down her cheeks.

We talked, we cried, we laughed. She shared her poetry; I sang a gypsy song to her—our favorite. This was my legacy—what she passed on to me—her need to write, to sing, to create…to survive.

It was beyond words, just feeling. Mama stood up, put on her coat and hat. There was a long, warm embrace and then she was gone.

"До свиданье, Mourechka," I heard her say. "*Until next time.*"

ELLEN NENNER

Ellen Nenner was a student at the High School of Music and Art, a piano student at the Juilliard School of Music, an Economics/Philosophy major at Mount Holyoke College, and received an M.A. in Urban Planning from the New School for Social Research. Formerly a writer and editor at the consulting behemoth McKinsey & Company, Ellen has attended writing workshops at the Fine Arts Work Center in Provincetown, Massachusetts, and is a trustee at MasterVoices, a not-for-profit performing arts institution that believes that the human voice is the world's most powerful instrument. Ellen has found a profound connection between telling stories through music and telling stories through the written word. She's currently at work on a non-fiction book of connected essays and short stories.

SO DOES SHE?

Ellen Nenner

I'm about ten when my mother decides I should go to charm school. I'm not sure what they do there, but I don't ask any questions. A few weeks later, she tells me we're going downtown to "Charming Debuts" this coming Saturday so I won't miss school.

We take the A train from Dyckman Street to 14th Street. The building is right next to the subway exit and the sign says Charming Debuts, 13thFloor, Room 3. We're shown into the office of the school's Director – Miss Eleanor Pitts. She stands as we enter, says hello, and points to the two chairs in front of her large, mahogany desk. She's skinny, has gray hair and doesn't seem very friendly. Once my mom and I are seated, Miss Pitts sits, folds her hands on top of the desk, and begins to explain what services the school provides to its "charm students."

As the conversation goes on, I learn that charm seems to have something to do with crossing your legs at your ankles rather than across your knees.

I don't look directly at Miss Pitts' face. Instead, I eye the wall behind her. It's covered with photographs of girls that don't look anything like I do. Some of them are older and some are about my age. Most of them are really pretty, with long, shiny hair and straight white teeth. My hair's not so great; it's kind of mousy colored. But I'm wearing my new gray wool dress and a pillbox hat on my head that my mother made me wear so I guess I look alright. I'm kind of scared, though. When I start swinging my legs back and forth under the chair, my mom gives me that *stop* look even though the Director probably can't see what I'm doing.

Mom answers all of Miss Pitts' questions so luckily I don't have to open my mouth. If I did, she'd see the wires that wrap around each and every tooth. She asks lots of things about me and the family, like what school do I go to, am I a good student, what does my dad do? Then she asks if I have any *"particular talents"* so my mother tells her that I play the piano and that Mr. Greenberg, my teacher, thinks I should try out for Juilliard.

"Would you like to go to Juilliard, Ellen?" the Director turns toward me and asks.

I'm forced to answer. I keep it short. "Yes," I say, hardly moving my lips.

Miss Pitts looks at me. After a few minutes, she stands up and tells my mother that she might be able to do more with me if I come back in a few years, without the braces.

Outside, my Mom and I walk to lunch at a nearby Horn and Hardart, my favorite restaurant. I already know what I'm going to eat because every time I go to an automat I have the same thing: creamed spinach, Harvard beets and macaroni and cheese. It's fun to put the coins in and open the little hinged window that holds each dish of food. I move my head close to the open glass-doored dispenser to get a glimpse of the person in the back who fills it up whenever it's empty

My mother doesn't say much on the subway ride home. I get the feeling she's disappointed at the way things turned out. I'm sure she took me to charm school because she thinks it's a good thing to do. *I want you to marry a prince*, she always tells me. Still, I can't help feeling sad that I'm so lacking in what she wants me to be that I need some sort of expert to fix me up. When we get out of the subway and walk toward home, my mother takes my hand. That means she loves me anyway, right?

ANNA PARET

Anna Paret is English and has lived in America for over twenty-five years. She has two almost-adult daughters, and lives with her husband in Larchmont, New York. Her work has appeared in a number of publications, including Ghost Town Literary Magazine, *Inscape*, and *Orbis*, and she has read several original stories at Read650's themed events. She is currently revising her novel and expects to be doing so for a while.

STRANGERS ON A BOAT

Anna Paret

The double-decked river cruiser lurched in its moorings as if already seasick. I hung onto the coarse rope slung along the gangplank, clutched my baby to my hip, and followed my father to a vacant wooden bench at the stern of the boat. Gripping the wrist of our jet-lagged, hyperactive toddler, my husband joined us to watch the last of the wedding guests arrive, and cast long shadows in the dragging midsummer evening. The River Thames slapped at the hull.

"There she is," Dad said. At the far end of the long barge, beyond the draping dresses and the high heels, the sparkling jewelry, and the black suits, my mother sat with her second husband Avi. Her sleeved, mid-calf dress covered her tightly clasped knees. Pearls strung her throat like a noose.

"She looks old," I said. It had been twenty years. Twenty-two. Mum had known Avi only a few months when she left England—left me and my siblings, children all of us—to move abroad with him. My sister had forgiven her, invited her to the wedding. I had neither seen nor spoken to her since she left. Handing the baby to my husband, I seized our buzzing two-year old by the hand. "I'll find somewhere quieter. Calm her down."

Below, I sat on a red, vinyl banquette under a porthole at the edge of the under-lit lounge. An engine kicked. The boat shuddered as if in protest, jerked, and settled into a barely perceptible cruise. My daughter, stretched out on the bench, pretended to try to fall asleep. Resting my hand on my child's belly, gently swelling with each breath, I told myself, "I will not spoil my sister's wedding; I will not confront Mum. Smile noncommittally if needed and ignore her; I will not spoil my sister's party."

The porthole darkened. The long evening finally accepted the night. Dance music filtered down from the upper deck and competed with the thrum of the engine: thud, thud. There was no way off this boat.

There was no way off this banquette. Mum and Avi, uninvited, dragged two chairs to the opposite side of my table, and sat down. "So tell me about yourself," Mum said. "What have you been up to?"

What have I been *up to*? For over twenty *years*? I don't think it was rudeness that prevented me from answering. She tried again, "It is very odd seeing your father. He looks older."

Mum smiled as if daring me to suggest that she did too. Her face seemed to break with the smile. The fine wrinkles which ran down her cheeks, from the corners of her bright-blue eyes, crevassed. "He has put on weight, your father. A lot." She patted her own, relatively flat stomach.

"Mmm."

"In fact I'm not sure I would have recognized him, if I hadn't seen him here. In context."

I had to know. I knew I might be punishing myself, but I had to ask. "Would you have recognized me?"

For a moment, she looked directly at me. Goodness her eyes were blue! I met her stare. Her gaze deflected and settled on my forehead. I held my breath.

"Probably not, no."

I didn't notice my husband descend the open-riser stairs. Shunting the baby to his other side, he slid across the bench and laid a protective arm across my shoulder, his warm thigh pressing against mine. "Are you okay?"

Mum and Avi rose from the table and walked towards the stairs. Avi paused, turned to me, and said, "You would like your mother."

I shook my head. "You don't know me. You can't possibly have any idea what—or whom—I like."

Mum and Avi returned to the dancing.

"Don't worry," I said to my husband. "I'll forgive Mum by the time my sister has her second wedding."

ELIZABETH PIMENTEL

Elizabeth Pimentel describes herself as being, in her youth, what her parents warned her against. She left her conservative family in Massachusetts to attend New York University. There she helped take over the university to protest the Vietnam War. In Washington, D.C., she was jailed for attempting to shut down the government. After college she joined a commune in Denver and drove a taxi. She received a physical therapy degree from the University of Colorado, and an MA in motor learning from Columbia. For the past thirty years she's taught neuroanatomy to medical students. She and her husband live in The Bronx, where they raised three boys. She's been published in the *Washington Post, Salon*, the *Daily News*, and others, and is currently writing a memoir about cab driving.

MY GRANDMOTHER, MY MIDWIFE

Elizabeth Pimentel

"You're having your baby at home?" my mother gasped when I told her my plan for delivering my third child. "You're forty-three – are you crazy?"

To quiet her I asked, "Where were you born, and how old was Nona when she had you?" The answer was at home on the farm in Plymouth, Massachusetts, at age forty-three. In fact, all of my Italian grandmother's ten children were born at home.

My first baby was born in a large urban hospital. I'd wanted the healthiest, warmest, drug-free environment for my child. But he was delivered in a cold, sterile operating room by emergency Caesarean section.

I swore it would be different next time.

Two years later, hoping to regain control in my second delivery, I switched to a smaller Bronx hospital and found a physician skilled at vaginal births after Caesareans – a rarity.

But the doctor's technique of squeezing the baby out by pressing on my abdomen every time I pushed, left me feeling like a used tube of toothpaste.

For my third delivery I wanted a secure, nurturing environment that would restore my power. I thought about Nona in her farmhouse in the winter of 1918, assisted at my mother's birth by her fifteen-year-old daughter Elizabeth, my namesake. I visualized my strong grandmother right after delivery giving orders from bed for my aunt to strip the sheets and soak them in the icy water of the nearby cranberry bog. It seemed simple back then to have your baby at home. It was way more complicated now.

Mine was a "geriatric pregnancy," the term for having a baby over age 35, which put me at risk for hypertension, diabetes, and miscarriage. My scarred uterus, a result of the Caesarean, raised the possibility of uterine rupture.

My older sister said, "Go to a hospital, where they can take necessary precautions." Well-meaning friends felt compelled to warn me of the dangers of homebirth. Still, I refused to view this pregnancy as pathological. I would take safeguards to protect myself and my child. And I would channel Nona.

Born in a village in Northern Italy, my grandma, who'd lived until ninety-four, had no formal education beyond grade school. She crossed the ocean with three small children in 1902, joining her husband in Massachusetts. Members of the community of Italian immigrants in North Plymouth came to her for advice. Nona was their midwife and had delivered many babies in their own dwellings.

Lacking that sort of approval from my peers, I devised a strategy for success by creating my own village with a support group of women who'd had previous c-sections and wanted vaginal births. Through them I found a doula to provide support and a certified nurse-midwife, with nearby physician backup, who would help me deliver in my Bronx abode. My husband and I took a course in birthing at home. I emphatically told the naysayers, "My grandmother gave birth in her own house ten times. I should be able to do it once."

Months later, in the throes of labor, I looked across my bedroom to my dresser mirror where I'd hung Nona's amethyst rosary beads, a cherished keepsake passed down to me. Conjuring up her strength, I gave birth to my healthy, nine-pound son. When my eldest child yelled out the window to the neighborhood kids that I'd had the baby, it was like the white smoke heralding the election of a new pope. I can't say I did it alone, because my midwife, husband, and doula were all attending to me while my children, watched by my sister's daughter, played downstairs. I can say I pushed my third baby out under my own efforts without medicinal, physical, or surgical interventions. I did it with the help of family and friends—an old-fashioned support system—like my grandmother before me. Sometimes, to move forward, it's helpful to go back to our roots.

JENNIFER RAWLINGS

Jennifer Rawlings is an award-winning writer, performer, and film-maker. In 2019 she won both the Karen Cushman Late Bloomer Award and Los Angeles' Sue Alexander Grant for her soon-to-be published novel, *Empty*. She's appeared on Comedy Central, CMT, PBS, VH-1, A&E, CNN, HLN, *I Am Battle Comic*, and two TEDx talks. Jennifer's solo show, *I Only Smoke in War Zones*, was featured at the "Humor for Peace Festival." In 2014 Jennifer was named one of " 21 Leaders for the 21st Century by Women's E News. Her directorial debut: *Forgotten Voices: Women in Bosnia* (Amazon) was screened at film festivals and universities worldwide. Jennifer has written for the *New York Times*, change.org, the *Wall Street Journal, Readers Digest*, as well as for television and film.

MOM IN A WAR ZONE

Jennifer Rawlings

I'm a mom. I have four biological children and one by marriage—my husband. For twenty years I have been traveling to war zones to entertain the troops as a stand-up comic. I've traveled to over seventy countries, doing over 350 shows for the military. I've performed in countries like Iraq, Afghanistan, Bosnia, and Kosovo.

There are two questions people always ask when they find out I travel to war zones to entertain the troops. The first question is "Aren't you scared traveling to a war zone?"

Yes, I am scared. I have zero military training, and I hate to fly.

The second question people ask is "don't you miss you kids when you travel? "No, I do not miss my kids. If I only had one kid, I probably wouldn't be so motivated to travel—but honestly with four kids I need the break.

I call my kids every single day from the phonebank at whatever base I am on, but it's difficult for them to call me. Cell coverage in Iraq and Afghanistan is patchy.

I remember one day, just outside of Fallujah, Iraq. The military base where we were performing was under heavy enemy fire. Mortars were dropping in the distance, the power was knocked out, flickering embers lit up the evening sky, a soft breeze carried the smell of eucalyptus mixed with the sharp acrid smell of bombs exploding.

The clatter of two Black Hawk helicopters with their rotor blades still chumming was several hundred feet away. These helicopters were waiting to fly us to Babylon, Iraq.

Black Hawks always fly in pairs. So far on this tour all the comics and our military hosts would be in one Black Hawk and our bags would be in the second Black Hawk. Tonight, everything was different – we were going to be flying "lights out so the insurgents couldn't see us; the local rebels were shooting anti-aircraft rocket launchers.

As soon as we got off "stage", tonight's stage was a flatbed truck, we ran to the chopper ducking our heads because the blades were running to ensure a faster take off. As I started to climb in the first chopper the military host pushed me and the three remaining comics into the second chopper. I'm sure the military split us up to cut their losses if something happened.

My heart was racing, my breathing heavy as I took my nylon jump seat in the chopper. The pilot and the co-pilot were performing a preflight safety check as I buckled my harness and closed my eyes in fear.

Moments later, I was jolted alert by a buzz, and a vibrate-"*what's that noise ? Oh my God it's my phone!*"

"Hello" I said my hand still trembling.

"Mom—it's Noah," Noah said, crying.

I could feel the blood leaving my face—I had given my kids strict instructions to only call me in an emergency. "*Who's hurt? Who's dead? What's on fire?*" My mind raced.

"Elijah ate all the Cheez-Its!" Noah was gulping his words.

"What?" I asked in disbelief. *Surely my middle son is not calling me in Iraq to complain about his little brother eating all the snack food.*

"Elijah ate all the Cheez-Its you bought. I didn't get any." Noah sobbed "Will you go to the store and buy me some more?"

I took a deep breath. What I wanted to say was, "*Why can't your dad ,who is probably sitting in the den, on the couch, watching golf, go to the store and buy you some Cheez-Its. I'm eight thousand miles away being shot at; he's eight feet away watching someone putt.*

But like most moms I bit my tongue and said, "I love you Noah—of course I will buy you more Cheez-Its."

LINDA SHAPIRO

Linda Shapiro attended Boston University and The New School and received a BA degree In English from the College of New Rochelle. She studied modern dance at the Martha Graham School of Contemporary Dance in New York City and taught modern dance while raising her daughters. Linda eventually had a business career in the outdoor industry and travelled abroad as an importer while writing, always writing, wherever she travelled. Linda takes writing classes at the Writing Institute at Sarah Lawrence College and writes with The Scarsdale Library Writing group. Her fiction, "At the Beach," was published by Forth Magazine.com, and she was honored to read "Chicken Soup for Howie" at Read650's *Stonewall+50* event at City Winery in New York City.

MOTHER LOVE

Linda Shapiro

"Did your mother hug you?" My adult daughter asked me. I took a few sips of coffee, stalling for time. I realized she might be thinking I wasn't affectionate enough. Could it be my mother's fault? Not wanting to betray her grandmother, who died before she was born, I hesitated to portray my mother as unloving. I'd learned to accept what I didn't get and appreciate what she was able to give me. I don't remember hugs, kisses or hand holding. I do remember her touching me when she cleaned my ears when I was little. I sank back to enjoy the feel of her fingers probing my ear and the scent of Shalimar floating in the air, the feel of her body next to me.

As I got older, I watched my mother in the kitchen, sipping hot water with lemon at the counter. Sometimes I watched tears fall down her cheeks. She was in bed a lot, mostly propped up on pillows reading. Always reading, books piled next to her bed. Maybe that was when I started reading in my green corduroy chair.

"She thought about me, that much I know." I told my daughter. "My mother was mostly quiet yet listening."

I was listening, too. One morning while coming down the stairs I stopped to hear my mother and father shouting. I sat on the steps and watched as my father threw dollar bills at her. Like dried leaves, they floated to the kitchen floor. My mother bent over, tears streaming down her face as she scooped up the money. After my father left, I went into the kitchen and picked up my juice glass without looking at my mother. She raised her teacup as though she didn't see me, then yelled, "Take your toast." I took the burnt toast and dashed out the back door. I ran to school. I tried to forget my mother's tears. When I came home she was peeling potatoes and carrots, then dropped them into a large pot of soup greens that boiled on the stove. I saw beads of perspiration on her face, but no tears. She poured some soup in a cup for me to taste. "She took care of me." I told my daughter.

One night, my mother came into my bedroom to find a mosquito that buzzed near my bed. I had yelled for her. I was seven or eight. When she came into my room she bent over me. Her bathrobe was wrapped loosely around her. I lifted my head to tell her a mosquito was buzzing in my ear. She put a light on, and then I heard the swat and knew the mosquito was dead. I like to think she pulled the blanket around me before she left, maybe gave me a hug, but I would be making that up. But the mosquito was gone.

Another day, in the kitchen, the linoleum floors were shiny from a new coat of wax and the spring rhubarb boiled on the stove. My mother showed me the Charleston. Her legs kicked like a showgirl. Her body moved like an easy piece of string in time to a silent rhythm that only we could hear. I fell in love with dance. My mother took me to see Margot Fonteyn dance *Swan Lake*.

My daughter and I sat for a long time at the kitchen table that day when she asked me about my mother. "She loved you?" I nodded. "My mother married at sixteen. She never had a chance to realize her dreams. She gave them to me." My daughter ate the hard-boiled eggs I made for her. I packed some chicken and vegetables left over from the night before for her to take home.

I hugged her tightly before she left. I hope I've hugged her enough.

LEANNE SOWUL

Leanne Sowul is an award-winning writer and music teacher whose work has appeared in such places as *Rappahannock Review,* Hippocampus, Mothers Always Write and *Confrontation,* and her live readings include Read650's *Gratitude* show at Lincoln Center. As an elementary band director, Leanne can play every woodwind, brass and percussion instrument (just don't give her a cello) and has directed over two hundred student performances. In 2017, Leanne won both the Scott Meyer Award for personal essay and the All-American Dream Champion Award for music teaching. Leanne lives with her husband and two children in the Hudson Valley. Connect with Leanne at www.leannesowul.com

THROUGH THE MIRROR

Leanne Sowul

My two-year-old daughter—wobble-kneed, shiny tap shoes clanking and pink backpack thumping against her bottom—toddles into the dance studio for her first class. The instructor lines up eight girls in leotards and skirts of pink, purple and black, all wearing shoes that make fun noises but occasionally slip surprisingly under their tiny feet. All of the girls are adorable, but I can't take my eyes off my Eleanor, whose pigtails swivel from left to right as she takes in the scene: the other dancers, the mirrored wall, the wooden barre just her height. She puts her hands on her hips and wiggles back and forth, her skirt lifting in the breeze, her smile radiating joy. Behind the one-way mirror that allows parents to observe without distraction, my throat is contracting with a fierce emotion that I can't release without attracting the attention of the other dance moms, chatting casually with babies hitched on their hips and coffee cups in hand.

I think of a photo that captures the moment my father first saw me in my wedding dress. He's embracing me. As his chin comes to rest on my bare right shoulder, his hands circling my waist, the camera zooms on his face. His cheeks and forehead are deeply creased under the strain of suppressed emotion. He is holding back tears. The camera sees it all, while I, the bride, am shielded from the moment by my dad's right shoulder. Just as the one-way mirror now shields me.

After a few minutes of tapping and "waving hello" with their toes, Eleanor and her classmates run to change into ballet slippers. Colorful scarves are handed out, and soon eight toddlers are twirling around the room to the strains of "Let it Go." Eleanor throws her scarf into the air and laughs as it floats gauzily down on her head. She runs to the mirror and presses her face into the glass, then whirls around to follow another girl on her tiptoes.

Only one year ago, Eleanor wasn't yet walking. Two years before that, while she was still in utero, a series of ultrasounds diagnosed her with a birth defect. Inside her abdomen, a set of extra tubes started in her kidneys and led nowhere, putting her at risk for multiple infections. At five months old, she had laparoscopic surgery to re-implant one tube; at fifteen months, a six-hour surgery reconstructed her ureters and bladder. As time went by without hitting her physical milestones, our pediatrician suggested blood tests, neurologists, physical therapy. My husband and I watched, despairing, as our daughter continued to crawl through life. Would she ever walk? Would she run?

Finally, on her twenty-one month birthday, Eleanor took a shaky step into her brother's arms. It's been less than a year since then, but watching her through the dance studio mirror, no one could imagine the stages— ultrasounds, anesthesia, belly scar, physical therapy— that led her here.

I have stages, too, that sound similar in a list. It started with a thyroid cancer diagnosis when I was fourteen and laddered from there: throat surgery, infected lymph nodes, radioactive therapy. For four years, my parents watched, despairing, wondering whether I'd meet my milestones. Would I go to college? Would I marry? Would I have children of my own?

I watch my daughter tap, point and tumble, and I think about that photo of my dad and the moment of his emotion veiled from my view. Ten years after cancer, his daughter stood before him in a white dress: a milestone met. The past would have rushed up to meet him, choking his throat in the way mine is choked now. The list would have run through his head as it runs through mine: ultrasound, anesthesia, belly scar; cancer, surgery, throat scar.

My finger blots a tear my daughter will never see. Through the mirror, she twirls on.

MARIA TERRONE

Maria Terrone's debut collection of nonfiction, *At Home in the New World*, was published in fall 2018 by Bordighera Press. Its opening piece was named a notable essay in *Best American Essays 2019*. Her nonfiction has appeared in such publications as *Witness, Green Mountains Review, The Common,* and *Litro* (U.K.). Also a poet, Terrone is the author of the collections *Eye to Eye; A Secret Room in Fall,* for which she won the Robert McGovern Collection Prize; *The Bodies We Were Loaned,* and a chapbook, *American Gothic, Take 2.* Magazines including *Poetry Magazine* and *Ploughshares* and more than 25 anthologies have featured her Pushcart Prize-nominated work. In 2015 she became the poetry editor of the journal *Italian Americana.* www.MariaTerrone.com

THE BODY BREAKING AWAY

Maria Terrone

I don't like to see what ninety-five years has visited upon the body that birthed me or feel the papery forearm that used to push a walker. But I see and feel and know: this is the same woman, now reduced to 57 inches, who used to hike a mile to a promising flea market, her swift stride communicating happy purpose.

"Her bones are so fragile, they're almost invisible on the x-ray," one doctor said.

Hearing that, it shouldn't have surprised me that a fracture was diagnosed again, a year after my mother fell at home, breaking her femur. "This is a tough one," the famous director of orthopedic surgery said, viewing the latest x-ray. And with those five words, my hopeful heart capsized. The bone never healed properly, he explained, and a four-hour surgery to fix the problem would obviously be very risky.

The safe alternative: live housebound with a permanently fractured hip. Legally blind in one eye for most of her life and now hard of hearing, my mother spends her days seated at a dining room table. From there, she observes wind in the trees. She rarely complains, but is surely in pain despite medication, wincing when she shifts her body in the chair.

Lately I've been thinking a lot about bones—how the diminishing flesh of the elderly makes them "no-bodies," near-phantoms not seen but looked through, practicing to be just bone.

The cliché is true: I've become my mother's mother. Shopping for her, cooking, paying bills, dealing with doctors, pharmacy, ambulette service, insurance company; hiring and scheduling her aides, updating the many women I meet in our neighborhood who say, "How's Connie doing? I miss her."

I dimly remember being fed almost-raw eggs from a pink Melmac cup and the taste of the liquid vitamin my mother spooned into my mouth. Now in my own kitchen I prepare vast quantities of chicken à la king, breaded cutlets, and tuna patties to stock her freezer. I recall how she over-bundled me as a child. Now when she feels the cold right through to her bones, I help her into the sweater I bought in size extra small.

My mother was always a worrier, and although she often forgets recent conversations, her frequent expressions of concern are clear. "I'm your mother," she declares by way of explanation—"Mother with Furrowed Brow" a universal archetype in her world view.

What's changed is my worrying about her when I never did before. Her firm opinions and her quickness had demonstrated self-confidence and independence. Now I wonder about her psychological and emotional states. How hard it must be for her to sit indoors in a wheelchair, giving up her daily walks to buy Lotto tickets and supermarket-hopping for the weekly specials. Knowing she'll never again socialize with her flea market friends—the gay antique dealers, the church ladies, the vendors who all knew her by name. To have only the memory of sifting through jewelry like an archaeologist searching for buried treasure who comes up, literally, with gold.

And I worry about her physical state. What's her blood pressure? Is she losing weight

despite her daily dose of Ensure? I can't know because it's too dangerous for her to stand, broken-hipped, on a home scale.

Her body is inevitably breaking down. Caring for my mother is facing myself several decades from now—that is, if I've inherited her gene for longevity.

In an old photo, my mother's dress clings to her curves. "You've got some body," uncouth men probably called out (a city girl through and through, she was never a homebody). As a teen in the era of mini-skirts, I'd hear her rebuke: "You're showing too much skin!" Now my mother must forego modesty as aides towel her back after a sponge bath, her wing bones prominent as if pushing through her body, and away.

MERCY TULLIS-BUKHARI

Mercy Tullis-Bukhari is a poet, essayist, and fiction writer whose writing focuses on the female experience through individuality, motherhood, and sexuality. She is a Callaloo Fellow, an MFA recipient in creative writing from The College of New Rochelle, and the Poet Laureate of the New York University Thirtieth Anniversary Celebration Gala. Mercy was named one of the "8 Authors Bringing Afro-Latina Stories to the Forefront" by Remezcla magazine and was a Pushcart Prize nominee in 2016 for her essay, "Black Dolls for Everyone." Mercy lives in New Rochelle, New York, with her two children. You can learn more about her at www.MercyTullisBukhari.com

WHEN MAMI PUT A GUN IN MY HAND

Mercy Tullis-Bukhari

While vacationing in Honduras with my mother the summer when I was eleven years old, the country was experiencing an energy crisis. All electricity was shut down by 8pm, and the humid heat made us sleep in only our panties since we did not have the electricity to operate a fan at night.

No electricity had also enabled the crime rate to sharply increase in the midst of pitch-black night. The energy crisis had lasted for several years, and the houses in our coloñia were getting broken into—and residents attacked—more often than they had ever been. The Honduran authorities did little to nothing to ensure safety. Adding to the problem, my mother was also a black woman from America who owned property. Coming from a country where roads were supposedly paved in gold and money grew on trees, she knew that if anyone in her coloñia was going to be robbed, it was going to be her.

In this time of lawlessness and disorder, my brother felt that guns needed to be in the house. He kept two hand guns locked in a chest that was hidden under my mother's queen-size bed.

When my mother was in her early twenties, she was a teacher who worked in the unmapped parts of the countryside of Honduras. While walking through the bush to get to a road, several men attempted to attack her. Knowing that she was lucky to have escaped, my mother vowed then that she'd be better prepared the next time men would attempt to assault her. She began to ride a motorcycle, taught herself how to use a gun, and always kept one in her workbag.

Our second night that summer, she shook me awake to tell me she heard something. The noise could have been the neighbor's chickens or the breeze from the nearby beach causing the coconut tree branches to hit each other and the roof of our house. Or maybe, actual intruders. My mother erred on the side of caution. Both of us, in our panties, her breasts hanging down and jiggling as she gingerly got off the bed and went on her knees to get the small chest from under our bed. She checked both guns to see if they were loaded. After checking each gun, my mother handed the smaller one to me. My hand was shaking because the power I held was overwhelming for my eleven-year-old mind and body. I feared accidently pulling the trigger and shooting my mother.

She saw my nervousness, so she grabbed the barrel of the gun and placed it on the windowsill for stability. She whispered, with the strength that only a mother who was protecting her child with unwavering urgency would say, "When I tell you to shoot, you shoot." She then turned to the window and yelled into darkness, "We have two guns pointing at you. Leave my property now, or we will shoot until we know you are dead!"

We stayed by the window for some time, until the sound that only she heard stopped. She took the gun from my still-shaking hand and put both guns back in the chest. She told me to go back to sleep, but I did not sleep that night. My eyes were closed, but my mind was alert with the image of my holding a gun, our chickens picking at dead bodies in our backyard, and thoughts of my mother not surviving an accidental shot.

I have not held a gun since. My mother and I never spoke about that moment. But that dark night my mother taught me that fear is a creation of the mind; and regardless of the threat, pushing through fear is key to survival.

SARAH BRACEY WHITE

Sarah Bracey White is a writer, teacher, storyteller and sought-after motivational speaker. She is a graduate of Morgan State University and the University of Maryland. Her published works include *Primary Lessons*, a memoir; *The Wanderlust*, a South Carolina folk tale; and *Feelings Brought to Surface*, a poetry collection. The *New York Times*, the *Journal News*, the *Scarsdale Inquirer*, and the *Afro-American Newspapers* have published her essays which also have been included in the anthologies *Children of the Dream; Dreaming in Color, Living in Black and White;* and *Heartscapes :True Stories of Remembered Love..* She and her husband live in Ossining, New York near the Hudson River, which is an ongoing source of inspiration for her. Sarah is a frequent contributor to Read650.

MY OTHER MOTHER

Sarah Bracey White

My father was blacklisted from teaching because of his efforts to get equal pay for colored teachers in our South Carolina hometown. I was just nine months old, but my mother needed to return to teaching. Reluctantly, she accepted her oldest sister Susie's offer to care for me, in Philadelphia, until I could go to school. Aunt Susie was married, with a successful home laundry business, but childless once again after the recent death of her adopted daughter. Aunt Susie relished my lively nature, talkativeness, and my interest in everything and everyone on Smedley Street.

My first memory is of the workroom in the basement of Aunt Susie's row house. I'm about four years old, standing at one end of a long, wooden table dressing and undressing paper dolls. She's at the other end, stacking freshly ironed sheets and pillowcases into bundles, securing them with brown paper and sealing the bundles with Kraft tape that she moistens across a shiny metal dispenser. She's singing Billie Holiday's "God Bless the child Who Has His Own."

Aunt Susie's skin is smooth and dark brown. She says it got that way from drinking her coffee strong and black, just like she is. She lets me drink coffee but always puts plenty of milk in mine - to keep me from getting dark like her, she says. She laughs when I tell her that I want it black, so I can be just like her when I grow up! "You sure won't have to do the work I do," she tells me. "You're going to college!"

During the summer, men with big, box cameras hooked on long legs often come to Smedley Street to take children's pictures. Aunt Susie says it's because they know the home-owners on our block of colored and white people have enough extra money to pay for pictures of their children. Aunt Susie always buys the pictures they take of me.

The summer I'm five and a half, my Mama sends for me to return home to South Carolina. "I don't want to go," I tell Aunt Susie. "I don't want you to go, either," she says, "but your Mama wants all her children home with her. You're hers, not mine." Memories of my life with Aunt Susie sustained me long after we parted.

From afar, Aunt Susie became my single-parent-family's guardian angel. When one of us was sick, she wired money for the doctor and medicine. Sometimes the money orders she tucked in her letters paid the light bill, or the rent. If my sisters or I needed something extra for school, or after-school programs, all we had to do was write to Aunt Susie. Soon, a box or letter would arrive bearing the requested item, or money for it.

My mother died during my senior year of high school. Days before graduation, I received a letter from Aunt Susie. In it were a train ticket, a twenty-dollar bill, and a brochure for a girls' camp in Vermont where she'd gotten her friend to give me a summer job as her kitchen-helper.

Aunt Susie beamed at my college graduation. "See, you made it! Just like I told you," she said, grinning proudly. Years later, when I self-published a book of poetry, Aunt Susie requested two dozen copies and sold them to her neighbors, and my friends, on Smedley Street. Her check for $196 came along with a note that read: "I'm so proud of you. Can't wait until your next book comes out. One day you'll be famous."

"I can't ever be famous," I wrote back. "Stories about famous people always include lots of pictures. I don't have any." The next time I visited her, Aunt Susie handed me a box of photos taken during the five years I lived with her. "Now," she said, "you don't have any reason not to be famous."

EDWARD McCANN
Read650 Founder

Edward McCann is an award-winning writer/producer and the Founder and Editor of Read650, celebrating the spoken word with live events in New York City and elsewhere. A regular feature writer for *Milieu* and a longtime contributing editor to *Country Living*, his features and essays have been published in many literary journals, anthologies, and national magazines, including *Better Homes & Gardens, Good Housekeeping, The Irish Echo, The Sun*, and others. His essay, "Pregnant Again," was selected for *Listen to Your Mother*, an anthology published by Penguin. He lives and writes in a pastoral spot about eighty miles north of New York City and is at work on a collection of essays about life in the Hudson Valley.

ACKNOWLEDGMENTS

First—and from the bottom of our hearts—a great big thank you to all the mothers everywhere. For everything.

Read650 is a nonprofit literary organization whose mission is to promote writers through curated live and digital performances celebrating the spoken word. Printed collections like this offer us additional opportunities to serve our mission, and I'm grateful to all the writers who submitted their work for consideration for this volume; I'm especially thankful to the exceptional writers whose work we've featured on these pages.

For their help in curating this volume, my thanks to Read650 editors Steven Lewis, David Masello, Karen Dukess, and Lisa Donati Mayer. Each of these talented writers reads dozens of submissions on each theme, communicating with the writers and each other as they work to help present the strongest pieces for production and publication. I'm grateful we share a passion for the written and spoken word, and I thank each of you for your commitment and generosity.

My sincere thanks to advisory board member Sara Caldwell whose marketing savvy and technical proficiency with the internet is helping Read650 better serve its mission each day. Thanks, too, to Angela Derecas Taylor for making that fateful introduction.

I'm thankful for the enthusiasm and hands-on assistance of our first-ever Read650 interns, Kerry Lubman and Olivia Prestia. Your contributions are helping our organization to grow, and I hope you'll remain part of our family.

Finally, my gratitude to nonprofits consultant and strategist Susan Ragusa—my nonprofit fairy godmother—whose free monthly Nonprofits TALK strengthens the nonprofit community through workshop and trainings addressing common organizational challenges. learn more at www.**SusanJRagusa.com**

READ650.ORG

INFO@READ650.ORG
FACEBOOK.COM/READ650

www.ingramcontent.com/pod-product-compliance
Lightning Source LLC
Chambersburg PA
CBHW072028170626
46811CB00008B/2992